"When it comes to finding God in c[...] better than Christie Purifoy. Her w[...] when I was unable to connect with [...] personal journey to find home turr[...] tive pilgrimage for my own soul. T[...] and wandering, and Christie Purifoy's smart, grounding voice is a new favorite."

—**Emily P. Freeman**, author of *Simply Tuesday*

"I have been terrified of hope. Because if hope disappoints, does that mean God is also a disappointment? Christie reminds us that hope, like dreams, is made of stronger stuff. She invites us into a year of her life lived in real time in an old Pennsylvania farmhouse, chock-full of hope and decay, promise and weeds, work and wonder."

—**Lisa-Jo Baker**, author of *Surprised by Motherhood* and community manager for (in)courage

"In *Roots and Sky*, Christie Purifoy paints an elegant expression of the church calendar—Advent, Lent, and Ordinary Time—with great depth of thought, expression, and insight. Planted in the rich soil of everyday liturgy, *Roots and Sky* is an astonishing, rhythmic work of unmatched artistry. There is no doubt: this book is a must-read for the lover of the quiet, contemplative, and beautiful.

—**Seth Haines**, author of *Coming Clean*

"This is not a book. This is a sanctuary. I met God here, in the hushed and unrushed space that Christie Purifoy has so exquisitely created for us. With a lyrical pen, Christie lights the candles, prepares the altar, and helps us see the sacredness of our everyday moments. Step inside and breathe again."

—**Jennifer Dukes Lee**, author of *Love Idol*

"*Roots and Sky* is the best kind of read: it reached me, passively and deeply, as I got lost in the pages. Christie ushered me into my own heart, through the back door, as she invited me across the foyer and into the rooms and out onto the sprawling green lawn of her one hundred-year-old farmhouse. God met me at Maplehurst too."

—**Sara Hagerty**, author of *Every Bitter Thing Is Sweet: Tasting the Goodness of God in All Things*

ROOTS
AND SKY

A JOURNEY HOME *in* FOUR SEASONS

CHRISTIE PURIFOY

Revell
a division of Baker Publishing Group
Grand Rapids, Michigan

© 2016 by Christie Purifoy

Published by Revell
a division of Baker Publishing Group
P.O. Box 6287, Grand Rapids, MI 49516-6287
www.revellbooks.com

Printed in the United States of America

Library of Congress Cataloging-in-Publication Data
Purifoy, Christie.
    Roots and sky : a journey home in four seasons / Christie Purifoy.
      pages cm
    ISBN 978-0-8007-2666-9 (pbk.)
      1. Life—Religious aspects—Christianity. 2. Christian life. 3. Spirituality—Christianity. I. Title.
    BT696.P87 2016
    248.4—dc23   2015025371

Published in association with William K. Jensen Literary Agency, 119 Bampton Court, Eugene, Oregon 97404.

16 17 18 19 20 21 22   7 6 5 4 3 2 1

In keeping with biblical principles of creation stewardship, Baker Publishing Group advocates the responsible use of our natural resources. As a member of the Green Press Initiative, our company uses recycled paper when possible. The text paper of this book is composed in part of post-consumer waste.

For Jonathan,
who dreams with me.

Contents

Acknowledgments

I imagined writing a book would be a solitary project, but now, at the end of it all, I remember with gratitude all those whose wisdom, encouragement, and love helped transform my black-and-white dream into a full-color reality. Thank you.

To everyone at Revell, especially my editor Andrea Doering.

To Lisa-Jo Baker, because word-loving friends are rare and precious. Thank you for seeing the book in the book proposal and for introducing me and my idea to Bill Jensen.

To my agent, Bill, for your enthusiasm, your experience, and your eagerness to talk books, music, and gardens.

To Allison Duncan who read drafts and gave me the books that would shape my own, and to Amy Knorr who prayed with me, studied Scripture with me, and gave me the gift of fruitful conversation.

To the writers who shared generously of their editorial skill, their professional contacts, and their publication experience, especially Amy Peterson, Shawn Smucker, and Ed Cyzewski.

To those who first made room for my stories at the table, including Lisa Velthouse, Shelly Miller, and Sarah Bessey and those who continue to do so, including Kris Camealy and Jenni Simmons.

To the inspiring writers who have also become friends, especially Laura Brown, Summer Gross, and Kimberley Coyle.

To Chelsea Hudson, for the gifts of friendship and photography. To Julie Collins, for reading endless books with Elsa so that I could slip away and write.

To Courtenay Bowser, for bringing me cool water while I walked in the wilderness.

To Jessica Suk, Aimee Tucker, and Melissa Baird. How poor I would be without your friendship. To Kelli Campbell and Lisa Ulrich, my sisters and my first readers.

To my parents, Mark and Lexie Day and Tom and Myrna Purifoy, for everything, but especially for showing your children The Way.

To my children, Lillian, Thaddeus, Beau, and Elsa. Without you Maplehurst would be only a house, never a home.

To Jonathan, for making my dreams come true with love, hard work, and a table saw.

And, finally, thank you to the Maker of this wild, beautiful world. Thank you for giving me the one thing I desired most: a song to sing.

An Arrival
and a Setting Out

LORD, I love the house where you live, the place where your glory dwells.

Psalm 26:8

I first saw the house on a day of record-breaking heat. I suppose we never choose the day when our dream will come true. Just as we do not choose the precise place our dream will carry us. This Victorian, red-brick farmhouse did not look like the home of my dreams. That first, terribly hot day, it did not feel like it, either. But my dreams began rearranging themselves almost the moment I stepped across the smooth, worn stone of Maplehurst's threshold.

Did Jonathan open the front door first, or did I? I no longer remember, but I can see again that first glimpse of the dim front hall with its staircase turning up and out of sight. Before my eyes adjusted to the darkness, I only sensed the fans that sat moving heavy air from room to room. Every one of the tall, elegant windows was tightly closed.

Having now lived more than a few summers at Maplehurst, the first of them while heavily pregnant, I know to open the windows just before heading to bed. In the morning, I step through whatever cool night air we have managed to trap, and I shut each window with a heave. These thick brick walls can hold back a heat wave for three days.

But back then I didn't know a thing about keeping an old house cool in the summer. What I knew was the artificial hum of the central air-conditioning in our tropical split-level and the surprising dream that began to visit us in that lonely place. We called it the *farmhouse dream*, but it was always about so much more than a house. It was a vision of growing roots, cultivating beauty, and opening the doors to neighbors, wanderers, and pilgrims—near and far. It was a vision of home.

I see now that it was also a vision of heaven on earth. Of course, that sounds audacious. As if I imagined I might reclaim Eden in a vegetable patch. Yet all of us have prayed for something like this for thousands of years. As Jesus taught us, we pray, "Your kingdom come, your will be done, on earth as it is in heaven" (Matt. 6:10). What does the answer to this prayer look like? Just how much heaven do we get to experience on earth?

Before we followed the call of my husband's new job offer and hurriedly planned this house-hunting trip, the dream we were dreaming never made complete sense. I pictured a white-painted farmhouse. I saw a garden, a henhouse, and apple trees. I imagined sweeping views and lovely greenness in every direction. But I was also sure I wanted our home to be a gathering place. How could we open our doors to the neighbors if our only neighbors were grazing cattle?

It was a glaring, sunburned day when Jonathan and I first drove down the long avenue lined with ancient maple trees. It felt as if we were entering a land ruled by benevolent giants. As we drove, the giants tossed their cool green skirts, giving us glimpses of Amish carpenters in straw hats. They were tapping nails into the last of a neighborhood of new homes. Here was a farmhouse, but the farm itself had disappeared.

Most likely, we wouldn't even have visited that day if the farm were still intact. Despite my daydreams, ours was not a budget for extensive acreage or bucolic views. Instead of grazing cattle, we could see children on scooters and bicycles. We could see two-car garages and the raw wood of new backyard decks.

Built in 1880, Maplehurst is a square, red-brick farmhouse wrapped in a white-spindled porch. It sits at the top of a Pennsylvania hill surrounded by a small island of land. It is an inevitable location for a farmhouse, and the home's name, bestowed when the bricks were first laid and the trees were first planted, is equally as inevitable. *Hurst* is an ancient term for a small rise. Together, *maple* and *hurst* evoke the towering figures that circle the house and walk in pairs down the hill and all the long way to the road. Say the words a few times to yourself and you might hear the sound of the breeze as it moves through the silvery green leaves at the crest of the hill. The name *Maplehurst* secures the house to the ground on which it rests. It is a name, and it is a contract.

Once long ago, the wavy glass of the home's old windows framed a view of fields striped in red and pink and white. Once, perfume drifted through screen doors. This area's nineteenth-century farmers raised the usual crops to sustain their families and livestock, but they earned their living growing roses. Today, where roses once spread in cultivated rows, we see only builders' homes and polished sidewalks. A long, looping, split-rail fence separates what is left of the farm from our neighbors' newly seeded lawns.

I felt my dream of home become reality as surely as I felt the heavy air blanketing my skin. Air like this feels like a burden. In the same way, my vision was no longer a pristine daydream. It acquired heft as I touched the warm wood of the banister's graceful curve. It seemed suddenly as weighty, yet still as welcome, as the baby girl sleeping in my belly.

I stood on the stairs trying to catch my breath, the air too heavy for my lungs, and I should have known. I should have recognized the moment for what it was. I had arrived at both the beginning and the end of a journey. I was right to believe that I had come home. I was right to imagine that my dream was being realized in this undreamed of place. But I was wrong to think that such a meaningful arrival could ever be accomplished in a moment.

A few weeks after moving in, one of my boys slid belt-buckle down and carved a deep scratch the entire length of that beautiful banister. Somehow I most clearly grasp the living reality of my dream come true when I touch that scratch or remember the miserable heat of that first day. We live in a good world shackled by decay. A world that always seems to fall at least a little bit short of its own promise. Yet glory dwells here too. Heaven and earth meet in scratches and scars. In broken banisters and in a Body broken for us.

Yet I had no interest in going back. When face-to-face with the very thing for which we have longed and prayed, what else can we do but press on deeper and farther? This is the only way to find him. This is the only way to find the one who created us as dreamers to begin with.

This is the story of my journey home. This is the story of a kingdom come. It begins with a full moon, the birth of a baby, and a September breeze that told us our years of wandering were finally at an end.

AUTUMN

The Writing on the Wall

Give me a sign of your goodness.

Psalm 86:17

There is a single, tall window at the very center of this house. It is above the landing that sits, like a hinge, between the first and second floors. For most of our first day at Maplehurst, I hardly glance at it. By the time the moving van pulls away, the sun has begun its slow downward drift. Gradually, the window recedes into shadow.

Lillian, Thaddeus, and Beau fall asleep on makeshift beds in their new rooms. Not long after, Jonathan and I climb toward our own half-assembled bed. We are tired. Worn out both by this new beginning and by the wilderness wandering of the past few years. We climb the stairs with a limp. Weighed down by thoughts of every task that needs our attention the next day, we might have missed it. But there is no missing the cool light puddled at our feet.

Glancing up, I see the top sash of that tall window exactly framing a silvery full moon. The glass in the bottom sash is etched, and every line catches the light and transforms it. Though it is night

17

and fully dark, a rainbow arches right across the spiderweb cracks of the old plaster wall.

Our lives are stories built of small moments. Ordinary experiences. It is too easy to forget that our days are adding up to something astonishing. We do not often stop to notice the signs and wonders. The writing on the wall.

But some days we do.

The wilderness also has its signs. Like the pillar of cloud and the pillar of fire, these mark it as a special, though bleak, place. It is the place where God meets with us as we wander. It is the place where new dreams are born and old promises are renewed. It looks different for everyone. My wilderness was dotted with palm trees and edged with coquina beaches.

Two years before our arrival at Maplehurst, we had left the Midwest eager for new jobs, milder weather, and a house of our own with a real backyard. We were unprepared for the enormity of our losses. Good friends. Close-knit community. A meaningful connection with the work of our minds and our hands.

There was one lost thing, in particular. It was such a natural part of our prewilderness lives that I only ever recognized it after it was gone. In our northern city, we had lived a seasonal rhythm of summer festivals and winter sledding, spring baseball games and autumn apple picking. Our moments and our months were distinguished by the color of the trees, deep red or spring green, and the color of the lake, sparkling and playful in summer, menacing and dull in winter.

These things were the beautiful, sometimes harsh, but always rhythmic backdrop to our days. Time was like music. It had a melody. In the wilderness, the only thing that differentiated one season from the next was my terrible winter asthma. Without time's music, I became aimless and disconnected, like a child's lost balloon.

Wandering taught me to desire rootedness. In the wilderness, I began to long for a place where my heart and body could settle, free of striving, free of restlessness. A place where my feet could touch ground. A place where I could grow. Like a tree.

I do not think this is my dream only. Not everyone longs for life in the country. Not everyone feels affection for old houses. But whether we are homebodies or world travelers, we all long for the moment of arrival. We all dream of the rest and peace we imagine waits for us at the end of a long journey.

For years prior to our move, I heard a quiet but insistent promise: "See, I am doing a new thing!" (Isa. 43:19). These words have finally been unleashed from the confines of my Bible and my journal. I can hear them in the wind. I can see them wherever I look. I can feel them kicking up a rhythm in my belly. A new home. A new season. A new life.

But it takes time to unlearn habits of fear and worry and fuss. It takes time to learn how to see what is right in front of our noses. We have been eating manna for hundreds of days, but here I am, anxious because our kitchen has no refrigerator and the car that has just been unloaded from its trailer will not start.

This morning, as I signed endless papers with one hand while holding squirmy children with the other, I told the woman selling us the house that it was "a dream come true." I wanted her to know that the years she spent reviving a farmhouse once sold as-is at auction have been worthwhile. That we will carry forward the work she and her family began. And I meant what I said. Maplehurst is our dream come true.

As with any cliché, the words *dream come true* loom larger than their literal meaning. We hear them and imagine all sorts of happily-ever-afters. A dream come true is rainbows and blue skies. It is all problems solved. It is easy smiles and no more tears. In my dream come true, I am eight months pregnant as I stand on the porch directing the movers as they carry our boxes into the house. From my shady spot near the front door, I can appreciate the air's cool undercurrent. I tap my foot in time with the yellow leaves already dancing across the branches of the antique cherry trees.

It is a momentous beginning, but it unfolds gradually and with the usual complications. Box after box after box. We have arrived. We have come home at last, but I quickly become preoccupied preparing lunch for the kids, finding sheets and pillows for our first night, and battling the hornets sneaking out of the neglected wooden playset two-by-two.

Perhaps a rainbow is exactly the right image for this dream-come-true life. Noah is remembered as a man of faith because he built the ark, but to me, the real act of faith was lived out beneath that first rainbow. Noah surveyed the empty, post-flood landscape and did not collapse under the weight of his to-do list. Instead, he put one foot in front of the other and began, in faith, at the very beginning. Sure of what he couldn't yet see, Noah cleaned up the mud. He fed the animals. He planted a garden. He did this all by the light of God's colorful message.

Tonight, I stand halfway up the stairs, witness to the twin wonder of a full moon and a rainbow. What does it mean? It feels as if something beautiful at the heart of creation has revealed itself to me. It feels like an embrace.

I am so stunned by the magic of the experience that it takes a moment before I recognize how ordinary it is. A full moon. A rainbow. They are a common birthright. A shared possession. If not entirely predictable, they are regular and repetitive. But this does not weaken their significance. I am convinced the world is saturated with meaning. We trample messages like scattered leaves beneath our feet. If only we have eyes to see them. Ears to hear them.

Bathed in broken light, I recognize something essential about this place. Maplehurst is built around a double banner of promise. At its heart is the glory of a full moon and the assurance of a rainbow—signs anyone can claim. Jesus once said, "Blessed are the meek, for they will inherit the earth" (Matt. 5:5). That is the inheritance I long for. I want to observe the ordinary things of earth—the moon, the stars, the rainbows, even the yellow leaves of the old cherry trees—and receive their messages. To hear them say what every weary traveler, every earnest seeker, longs to hear.

Welcome home.

Birth and Rebirth

The LORD will write in the register of the peoples:
"This one was born in Zion."

Psalm 87:6

When I was pregnant with my first child, I wondered what it would
be like when I held her for the first time. I imagined love and joy.
I imagined awe. What I felt instead was surprise.

When the nurse placed Lillian on my chest, the first thought
to organize itself out of the jumble in my head was the obvious
observation: *this is a real baby*. The second was: *Who is this? I've
never seen this person before in my life*. I had carried her in my
body and in my dreams for so many months. Jonathan and I had
named her. I had already washed her clothes and folded them in
drawers. How could it be that she was a stranger?

This memory often returns to me. I think of it because I am
preparing to meet another little stranger; because I am, once again,
washing and folding tiny socks and shirts and blankets. I also think
of it because I am settling in to a house I call *home*, but this house
on the hill is unknown to me. In all the dreams I have dreamed in

23

the past few years, I never imagined that home, the true home I longed for, would feel so unfamiliar.

As I stumble around trying to decide where the bedsheets belong and where the board games should be stored, I feel anxious. I feel some fear I cannot identify, but I know it is entirely out of proportion with the task of emptying cardboard boxes.

The first time I heave up a bit of this ground with our old, dull shovel, I am startled by the density and brilliance of its orangey-redness. In this moment I gain a piece of knowledge I had never known was missing. I finally appreciate what my gardening books mean when they say *clay soil*. I suppose I have always pictured something like the quiet color of a sun-faded terra cotta pot. But this. This is alive. I've never seen anything quite like it.

It is possible that I have lived on similar clay before. I am ashamed to remember how many places I called home before I ever thought to dig beneath their surface skin of grass or gravel. Now I understand we can't ever truly know a place without the intimacy afforded by a spade.

I am uncertain whether I took my first steps on clay soil or sand, but I know I have long wondered if home is the place from which we come or the place we are headed. The estrangement I felt from my surroundings as a child growing up in Texas has always meant that I tend to see home as my end and not my beginning. When I was young, I dreamed of winters that bring snow and summers that don't imprison you for months at a time within air-conditioned walls. As an adult, I have learned that home is more complicated than climate.

I want to fit into Maplehurst like two perfect puzzle pieces snapping together. An easy fit would be like a sign. It would be evidence. It would be the proof that I am right to call Maplehurst my home. That I am right to invest so much longing and desire in this place. That I am right to plant my dreams in such unfamiliar dirt.

I want proof because I want hope. Life has been bleak these past few years. Like a long, hard winter. If I have come home, then surely life will get easier. Isn't that the meaning of spring? Every time I trip across the box spring that won't fit up the narrow, winding staircase to the third-floor guest room, when I fail to find a place to store the children's art supplies, or when I cannot figure out if those are weeds needing to be pulled or perennials asking to be mulched, I secretly wonder if the pieces will ever come together. If this is my home, then how long will it be until I feel at home?

At 11 p.m. on September 11, the pieces of my life suddenly form a frightening picture. All evening I had hoped my contractions might roll and roll and roll away, but now I know. I know our baby will come tonight, and I know there is no one to stay with our children. No mother or mother-in-law. No good friends or familiar neighbors.

We made plans for Jonathan's mother to fly in one week before our baby's due date. This, despite the fact that Beau, our third child, arrived a whole week overdue. I can remember every second of that agonizing wait. Perhaps because of the heaviness of that memory, I never expected labor to come before I was well and ready for it. I never expected our baby would arrive two weeks early.

But these contractions continue to break like waves, and the dark night grows darker, until, with Lillian, Thaddeus, and Beau already asleep in their upstairs beds, Jonathan calls the only person we can think of. The person who had said, "If you need anything . . ." and to whom we had replied, "Thank you! We're sure we'll be fine." We call the real estate agent who helped us buy this house.

I worry that three-year-old Beau will wake in the night and find a stranger in his parents' bed. I worry about the food my kids will eat for breakfast. I fret over the lunches they will need for school. Will Thaddeus be able to explain his food allergies? Will they remember what time the school bus arrives? And behind all the many worries, is my fear of well-remembered pain.

We speak frequently of our fear of the unknown, but it is our known fears that often make us stumble. Our child coughs, and we tumble down a black hole remembering last year's terrifying bout with croup. The plane lifts from the ground, and we suddenly feel in the pit of our stomachs the memory of that violent turbulence. We rarely feel stronger for having survived or overcome. We feel only despair. *I cannot possibly go through that again*, we tell ourselves.

Three times before, I have stared down the dark tunnel of a laboring night like this one. I remember feeling overwhelmed. I remember feeling afraid. I give memory a power it has no right to hold—the power to predict my future. I forget that God's promise of newness arrives with a command: "Forget the former things; do not dwell on the past. See, I am doing a new thing!" (Isa. 43:18–19).

When our agent steps quietly through the door, we give her a few instructions about breakfast and bus schedules and lunch sacks. We show her our bed. Then we say good night, hoping she can claim a little sleep. I know it is still too early to arrive at the hospital, but I don't want to wake the kids. "Let's walk," I say to Jonathan.

Shutting the front door with a tug, I pull my wrap just a little tighter around my shoulders. I tuck my arm into his and begin measuring the driveway that circles the house and heads out toward the road. Each step is one step away from my past. Each step is one step closer to something new.

In the first chapter of Genesis, the word *eres* is used to designate the whole earth. In the second chapter, where we find Adam and Eve at home in Eden, this word is not used. Instead, the word is *adama*, meaning ground or soil. Adam was made of *adama*. He was born from the ground beneath his feet, the very soil he cultivated. It is the origin of his name, and it is his home.

In silence, Jonathan and I walk loop after loop around a house I can still hardly believe is ours. I squeeze his arm when the pain arrives, but otherwise I count stars. There are so many stars. I am noticing lights far off in the neighbors' windows. I listen to autumn whisper in the cool breeze and owls greet the darkness from their hidden homes. I am being born again. Born to this new place.

As humans, we roam the entire world. We even venture beyond it into space. The whole planet is ours, but the whole planet is not our home. Instead, home is the ground we measure with our own two feet. And home is the place that measures us. Home is the place that names us and the place we, in turn, name. It feeds us, body and soul, and if we are living well, we feed it too.

Home is the place we cultivate with our love.

How does a square comprised of brick and wood and plaster become a home? How does an unimportant hilltop become sacred ground? Perhaps it begins, not with ease and comfort and a perfect fit, but with birth pains. Perhaps it begins when you have no choice. When you are so helpless all you can do is release your worry and your fear and watch as they float up and over three red-brick stories to join the stars. Like balloons. Or birds. Or prayers.

Our world is full of beautiful places. Our world shakes with the newborn cries of so many little lives. But they are not all given to us to name and to love. Of all the places to love, I have been given this old, red-brick house perched on its small rise. Of all the children to love, I have been given one daughter. Two sons.

And then, one more daughter.

We leave for the hospital just before one. Our baby, a little girl we do not know but whom we already love, is born just after four.

By six, Jonathan is home, welcomed by the lamppost that glows just beyond the shelter of the porch. He is flipping pancakes in the kitchen when our children wake and hear the news of what has happened in the night.

"You have a sister," he tells them. "Her name is Elsa Spring."

The Wanderer's Return

> Those the LORD has rescued will return. They will
> enter Zion with singing.
>
> Isaiah 51:11

We come home to Maplehurst again and again. First, on a blistering day in July. Then, the day we sign the papers and tell the movers, "Here please, upstairs please, through that door over there, thank you so much." And then we come home again, this time with a daughter named Spring. With each homecoming, I feel myself standing more steadily on the ground of our new lives.

We pose for pictures on the porch. While I had been blindly cleaning and unpacking, morning glories I did not plant crept up and over the white spindle rails. Velvety, deep purple flowers on a secret mission. They needed all summer to quietly reach this height. When we come home from the hospital with a sleeping baby in our arms, they are ready and waiting to dance around the edges of our first family photograph.

Elsa wears a delicate bit of pink and white softness, the kind of clothing the baby stores label a "coming home outfit." It looks so much like the homecoming gown worn by her older sister. Same colors. Same softness. But new.

I have lived something quite like this moment three times before. This fourth time feels like a memory even as I stand in the midst of it. The morning glories tumble at the edge of my sight, but I can already see how they will look frozen between the pages of an album. I can already imagine this pink and white dress folded away in a special keepsake box. It will sit on a shelf in the third-floor closet, gathering dust alongside those other boxes.

As a child I found autumn only in books or the construction-paper leaves we cut out to decorate our classroom windows. I left Texas at twenty in a rush to make up for so many lost Septembers. I pointed my camera at every giant pumpkin. I collected great armfuls of the most perfect autumn leaves and pressed them between the heavy covers of either my *Oxford American Dictionary* or Julia Child's great tome on French cooking.

Now I visit a local farm stand with Elsa wrapped tightly around my chest, and I remember autumn visits to other markets. I remember carrying other babies in slings so I could have both hands free for acorn squash and Concord grapes. I still search for those babies. I search in skinny limbs and freckled noses and tangled hair, but my babies are gone. They have been replaced by children who need to reintroduce themselves almost every day, so quickly do they change and grow.

During the years of my wilderness wandering, I couldn't think of fall without an ache. I see now how deep that ache extended. So much deeper than a longing for pumpkins on the porch or sugar maples catching fire. The wilderness was endless summer, but it was also the place where we disassembled our well-used baby crib. It was the place where I finally surrendered my long struggle with infertility. I can still see Jonathan, back bent and screwdriver in hand, while the palm tree outside covered the pieces of our crib with shadows.

In the wilderness, I said *thank you* for the three children I had been given and packed away special baby clothes, assuming I would only unpack them again for a grandchild one day. But the glory of autumn has come back to me. Or I have come back to it. And my arms hold another daughter.

My world feels fresh and new. As if it has been remade. Yet this newness doesn't displace the past. It grows out of it. Elsa looks so much like her sister that nine years disappear as I cradle her and sing old, familiar songs. New life and old memories sit together within the worn, wooden embrace of my white rocking chair.

On days like this, I feel sure life is a fountain. That our lives are not defined by what we've lost but by all that returns, fresh and new. A year before our arrival at Maplehurst I inked a small note in my Bible next to Joel 3:18. Where it says, "A fountain will flow out of the LORD's house," I wrote the words "Fountain House Dream." I do not know why I connected the image of a fountain to our farmhouse dream, but of all the houses we had visited that July day, Maplehurst was the only one with a fountain.

When I lean on the porch rail, I can see the depression in the circular flowerbed where that fountain once sat. The driveway runs straight from the road toward the house and the front porch, but where the avenue of maples ends, the driveway branches and a flowerbed sits just beyond this split. The two paths of the drive flow around the flowerbed and around the house until they meet near the back fence. The driveway looks like a needle, and the house sits tucked within its eye.

The flowerbed is a checkerboard of summer weeds and autumn mums. But no fountain. The sellers asked to take it with them, and we, desperate for a speedy closing date, said yes. "Find and install a new fountain" is scribbled somewhere on the many to-do lists we are always making and losing. Of course, it is ridiculous to dream of a fountain. It is not prudent to budget for a fountain when there are windows to repair, ancient bricks to tuck-point, and a heaving asphalt driveway to eventually replace.

Inspecting the driveway, I can see how the rate of decay has only increased now that two little boys are in residence. Where the asphalt is cracked, my sons have managed to pry out large chunks. The pieces are scattered about, ready to trip anyone walking in the tall grass nearby or give unsuspecting motorists a jolt.

Already in these first few weeks, I have observed several drivers take a wrong turn toward our house. Through the windshield, you can see the surprise and panic on their faces. It says, *Oh dear, this isn't a road. How do I get back to the street?* But the driveway is narrow and tree-lined, and it isn't really possible to make a U-turn. Watching them from a window, I wait to witness the moment when panic turns to relief. It is the moment they realize that the driveway turns, that it ties the house in an oval. Always, as they circle the back of the house, their faces settle. They relax, knowing that, though they move onward, they are really turning back.

Homecoming is a single word, and we use it to describe a single event. But true homecoming requires more time. It seems to be a process rather than a moment. Perhaps we come home the way the earth comes home to the sun. It could be that homecoming is always a return and our understanding of home deepens with each encounter. Somehow, with the birth of my last child, I have journeyed back and onward to my own beginning. I have a new song to sing, and it echoes with so many other songs I have loved. So many songs I thought were lost.

Our first autumn at Maplehurst is just beginning, but I can feel the clock of these days already counting down to that devastating moment when the last leaf falls. Or my last baby goes off to school. But the twelve months of the year hold this house just like the road around it. And nothing good is ever truly lost, which is another way of saying all is being made new.

A fountain is an extravagance. But extravagant things just may be the truest things. We fool ourselves if we believe that life is the tedium of our to-do lists broken up by occasional highs, like a baby's homecoming, and occasional lows, like that baby's first terrifying trip to the emergency room. Everyday life is utterly extravagant. It is morning glories we did not plant. It is four children we did nothing to deserve. It is moonlight and starlight, rainbow-colored leaves and autumn rain. It is the shelter of trees, the songs of birds, and the enduring sight of a farmhouse on a hill. It is more beautiful than it needs to be. It is more meaningful than we can begin to comprehend.

This life is a fountain. Not slipping away but pouring out, always carrying us deeper into the heart of things—to home.

Here Prayers Are Born

You hem me in behind and before, and you lay your
hand upon me.

Psalm 139:5

By summer's end we droop like tired sunflowers. We are browned by
the heat, and our heads are heavy with memories. Then, October.
Everything feels fresh again. The marigolds and zinnias pass the
baton of their colors on to the trees. The sky regains that clarity
of blue we only ever see in fall.

Autumn was only an ache, for all those months, tipping over
into years, when I wandered in a place without seasons. Now that
ache has become a vessel for the kind of joy we know only when
something precious has been lost and then found again.

I begin to find this lost season in patches—a spray of orange
leaves here, a vine suddenly running itself red. I see how each
season lies tucked up inside another. How fall's warm yellow is
hidden within summer's cool green. How even the scented explosion of spring lies sleeping within winter branches that seem
brittle with death.

35

I want to go for long walks in the woods. I want to drive up and down the green hills of this countryside, to dazzle my eyes with autumn glory. I want vistas. I want movement. I want to dive in the way my children tip themselves over into great piles of leaves. But Elsa is losing weight instead of gaining weight. She is moving in the wrong direction, and helping her requires that I stop moving.

Instead of long walks and longer drives, I hold her in the rocking chair. While she sleeps, I stay in that rocking chair, this time with my hospital-grade nursing pump. My movements shrink to the small triangle of the rocking chair, my bed, and the teakettle I keep humming in the kitchen.

From our four-postered nest on the second floor, I can see straight ahead toward a bow window. It is a three-part harmony of a view. The curved windows still hold their original panes. Though the glass is smooth to touch and clear like crystal, it washes everything it sees with waves. From where I lie with Elsa, October appears to be a kaleidoscope of yellows and reds, a magical view spun by antique glass.

I am grateful for the distraction of that carnival view. It takes my mind off Elsa's hunger. It turns my eyes from the peeling, flaking plaster of the bedroom walls. One of the first things I had hoped to do was repair the walls and repaint the interior of the house from top to bottom. I imagined that smooth, clean walls would be a balm in the early, blurry days of caring for a newborn.

It was a huge job, and we could not possibly do it ourselves in the brief time we had before Elsa's birth. Though we had never aspired to hire painters before, we succumbed to the tug of dream and desperation. We brought in a professional to give us his estimate for the work. I think Jonathan and I both knew that professional painters would cost a great deal, but the actual appraisal, when it came, was sobering.

The longer we spend in this house, the longer our to-do list grows. Where I want to do more, circumstances dictate that I do less. Without even discussing it, Jonathan and I both understand that we will do this work ourselves, and we will do it slowly. I will have to make my peace with faded colors and flaking plaster, at least for a while.

We live so much of our lives with our hands tied behind our backs. With everything to do—more than we can possibly accomplish in a day—we are yet further hampered by illness, tiredness, a lack of money or time. This seems true even on good days. With twenty-four hours in a day, how many must we devote to unproductive necessities like sleeping? Eating? Not to mention shopping for food or washing sheets or changing endless diapers. Some days we have more freedom than others, but we are always, to some degree, hemmed in by weakness, by need, by lack, or by loss.

We are as hungry and needy as newborn babies. We fool ourselves if we imagine anything else to be true.

When dusk creeps in, the kaleidoscope images flicker with gold stars. They are the lamps from our neighbor's windows and the floodlights over their back doors. I want to meet those neighbors. I want to paint my walls. I want to take great strides across my life. But I can do little but sit. Watch. Wait. *Why must it be like this?*

So many questions are bound up in that word *why*. I cannot understand why I am stuck in bed. I dream of hospitality, but I am burdened by a body unable even to feed my own baby. I dream of community, but there was no one even to visit me and Elsa in the hospital. I ate the maternity ward's "celebratory meal" of steak and cheesecake alone. My hospital room was too small for all six of us. I ate in silence while Elsa slept, sealed off by the plastic, wheeled cot.

In the wilderness, I wandered with very little sense of direction. My old dreams and plans crumbled, and new dreams grew up only very slowly to take their place. But having come to this new home, I am no longer aimless. I know exactly where I want to go. I can see a vegetable garden and a brood of chickens. I can see new friendships and special celebrations. I can see children and trees growing. I can see meals shared around a long farmhouse table. And I can see my feet planted on the ground while four seasons shift purposefully overhead. Each one arrives, departs, and returns in a sustaining rhythm. Yet I am held fast, unable to run toward the future as I long to do.

Do we make our dreams come true? Or do we only watch and wait, ready to embrace them when their time has finally come? Each night, as darkness begins to rise like a fog, my bedroom windows are transformed into mirrors. Gradually I can see my own staring face superimposed on October's golden beauty. Slowly, even the glittery stars of my neighbor's porch lights become harder to find until I am left with only my own wide eyes and the reflected glow of my small bedside lamp.

Only then do I lie down face-to-face with my small daughter, searching the far horizon of her forehead and the uncharted waters of her cheek. That is when I remember the wisdom of Genesis. I remember that each new day begins in evening. It begins when we let go and fall asleep. It begins with our dreams and God's work.

When we visited Maplehurst in July, we were welcomed by the fluttering green of a thousand, a hundred thousand, maple leaves. I looked at them and knew they would transform come fall. I knew this, but it was like a rumor from a far-off land, too impossible to believe. Of course, my dream was hiding in plain sight. It only needed autumn rains to wash the green away. I hope my dreams for this place are like those leaves. I hope the good things I am waiting for are already tucked up, hidden and waiting, within this place. Like one season waiting within another.

I am a prisoner, bound tightly by the beautiful answers to my own prayers. This lovely, hungry daughter. This special, crumbling house. Yet it is only when we are fenced in that we begin to know the true shape of ourselves and of our lives. What it is we long for. What it is we love. Hemmed in on every side, we begin to understand, *I am not enough*. Until every limitation and every need becomes a prayer. And every prayer a light revealing the treasure that is always, already ours.

These Days
without Name or Story

All the days ordained for me were written in your book.

Psalm 139:16

Though we managed to visit a few local churches before Elsa's birth, we take a break from church attendance during the first weeks of caring for her. I miss Sunday morning worship but am grateful for slow, quiet weekends. As I gather up my Bible and a few of my favorite prayer books, I can hear the children racing their bicycles through piles of leaves beneath my bedroom window. I want to remember where we stand in the church year.

Early autumn falls in the season of Ordinary Time. If the church calendar tells the full story of God's redemptive work, Ordinary Time seems somehow outside of the story. There is no drama, no central narrative. It isn't Advent, Lent, or Easter. The meaningful intensity of those special seasons is lacking. Though time passes, it doesn't feel as if we are on any kind of journey. The days simply *are*.

41

Ordinary describes these October days exactly, and it is the ordinariness that I so resent. The connection feels apt, though several of the books in my lap remind me that this season derives its name from the word *ordinal* rather than *ordinary*. These days of Ordinary Time are numbered: one, two, three; they do not tell a story. But I am on a journey toward realizing a vision, I am sure of it, and so I have no patience for ordinary. No patience for numbers plodding one after the other. I am restless in my rocking chair.

Yet if nursing Elsa leaves me with little time for productivity as I imagine it, it does leave me with hours for reading. I keep a stack of reading material on a little tea table at my elbow. I read Scripture. I read prayers. I read old mystery novels. I read every one of my gardening books. I read and reread the descriptions of daffodils and tulips in a catalog of spring bulbs, and I make occasional notes in Elsa's baby journal.

I have three other journals—one for each of my children—in various stages of incompletion. Even though I failed to answer every prompt and the record of each child's growth is spotty, the books themselves tell me that those days mattered. One day with a baby can feel exactly like so many other days. Months are lost in a blur of diapers and baths and nighttime feedings. Yet this ordinary sameness is worthy of being bound up between delicate cloth covers embroidered in baby pinks or baby blues.

Before moving to Maplehurst, God seemed to speak to me so often and so clearly. My Bible is scattered with ballpoint stars and inky underlines, whispers I once gathered in the wilderness. But the pillar of cloud and the pillar of fire departed. They brought me to this farmhouse on the hill and no farther. I feel as if I have stepped outside of the story. I feel stranded in Ordinary Time. I can no longer sense any narrative momentum. How will my dreams for Maplehurst be realized if I am stuck in some sort of eddy?

I long for the confident excitement of living out a story. I like to know I am quickly moving from point A to point B, from introduction to conclusion, and from puzzle to solution. I suppose I could argue we are never truly outside of the story. We never really pause in our journeys, as humans, as communities. Each second ticks by at precisely the same rate, regardless of whether or not it is swollen with significance. Yet I long to lift these seconds up like a strand of beads, each one in its place and the whole a thing of beauty. But no matter how hard I try, I cannot fit these ordinary days into some narrative mold or artistic form.

Ordinary days don't matter all that much, but they are given to us. God gives the extraordinary—the birthdays, the holidays, the moving-in days, the days when we come face-to-face with him on the mountaintop. He also gives the deep-valley days. Days in the valley of the shadow of death when, strangely, I have been more aware of his nearness than ever before. But as if these days were not enough, God gives us more.

I cannot tell whether or not these ordinary days are significant in the story of myself, in the story of my daughter, in the story of Maplehurst. Perhaps they are not. But can it be this lack of significance that makes them such a gift? They are gloriously excessive. Like a whole bowl of mismatched beads just asking me to thrust in my hand and wave my fingers. Like a sky spilling over with stars. Every moment I fail to record in Elsa's baby book is like an unseen galaxy or an unnamed planet. Created but unobserved. Made but unremarked. What are they for? Why does God make them anyway? For the joy of it?

He gives the blue-sky day in a month of blue skies. He gives the hand-holding day in a decade of holding our child's hand. He gives the sunrise and the sunset, always and again. He gives me a husband in the kitchen making breakfast. Not because it is Mother's Day or because we have a new baby, but because it is morning. Again, it is morning. Again, we hunger. Again, we are satisfied.

I abandon my stack of books and catalogs. I relinquish the pump and the herbal teas and the unanswered questions. I leave Elsa asleep in her bassinet and follow the narrow curve of the back stairs down toward the kitchen. I want to make sweet apple butter. Apple butter is less necessary than either apples or butter. I suppose it isn't necessary at all, but I love it. It tastes of cinnamon, cloves, and extravagance.

Beau helps by washing the same six apples over and over, his skinny little elbows deep in the farmhouse sink. I peel and chop. I measure out spices. I watch the pot of brown sauce bubble and pop. Making apple butter is like making applesauce twice. First, I cook the apples to the consistency of sauce. Then I stir in brown sugar and spices and cook it down a second time.

The irony of this double effort is that you end up with something much less practical than applesauce, a snack that is self-contained, lacking nothing, and always accepted by my picky little eaters. But apple butter offers something plain applesauce never can. When making apple butter, each bubble in the pot becomes a scented shooting star, and the air in my kitchen is soon heavy with cinnamon trails.

October is here, and I can no longer see very far ahead. But I am reading bulb catalogs. I am making apple butter. I am living a surplus of days that overflow with spring dreams and autumn flavors. And I am becoming convinced that the year is a book of life. The four seasons of God's creation tell untold stories, name unnamed things. They bind all that is special and all that is not.

This Is a Testimony

Come and hear, all you who fear God; let me tell you
what he has done for me.

Psalm 66:16

I have come home to a place made for storytelling. Stories lurk
especially in the dark corners of this house. I am sure the dusty,
black bowler hat we found tucked away on a shelf in the dirt-
floor basement has something to tell us. It looks like a hat made
for an elegant man, but it is, unaccountably, an exact fit for my
six-year-old son.

The basement must be saturated with old tales. I sometimes
think they echo against the deep stone walls of the original water
cistern. Peering into its dry depths, I can see a ladder propped
against the side, but my eyes cannot reach the spot where the bottom rung meets cool earth.

Stories also seem to rise from the root cellar's deep cave. The
root cellar shares a ceiling with the main basement, but its floor
is dug more deeply and can only be reached by following another
short flight of steps. When I bravely open the door at the top of

these steps, cold air lifts the hair on my arms even on the hottest Indian summer day.

Despite the basement's unmatched gloom, I hear most of these mysterious stories whispering outside the house, as I walk the edges of the property or drive the narrow country roads. In October, the weeping cherry tree across the street turns the color of a copper penny. When fog curls around the trunk, I half believe the headless horseman will pass by. Perhaps the bright sunshine of summer washes out shades from the past. Whatever the explanation, now that it is fall, I feel as if shadowy figures, old saints perhaps, move just at the edge of sight.

There is a farmhouse farther down our country road, on the other side of a small stream. It is even older than Maplehurst. Jonathan and I had the privilege to cross its threshold the day of our house-hunting trip. We found the original land deed framed on the wall, and it was signed "William Penn" in faded, spidery script. The agent who showed us that house explained that Hessian soldiers once camped on the fields nearby as they marched to join the redcoats. I feel I have seen their shadowy muskets between the trees.

Like so many of the homes in our area, that fieldstone house was built by Quakers. These practical colonists, the first to settle here, cleared their fields and then used the stones to build their homes right up against the roads. It would have been wasteful to give up any of their cultivated land for the vanity of a front yard. Now, when I slow to a stop at every four-way crossing, I feel as if the spirit of a silent Quaker housewife might still be watching from her parlor window.

A mile or so down our road, there is an old Quaker graveyard with too many tiny gravestones. Washing the special tubes and bits and bobs that deliver Elsa's supplemental formula, I think of that graveyard. I picture the old, smooth stones and the fresh, green grass. I acknowledge how different my story, Elsa's story, once might have been.

In spring and summer, I always find it difficult to accept the reality of death, but autumn in this countryside of old stone walls, covered bridges, and somber Amish horse-drawn buggies is working a subtle change in me. We live so much of our lives in places that seem to have no past. I find it nearly impossible to believe in death while crossing a vast parking lot or standing beneath the fluorescent lights of a warehouse store. But here, where the sign on a neighbor's farm says *1732* and the plaque beneath the spreading oak tree at the edge of our property is dated a hundred years before that, it sometimes feels as if we still share these fields with those who cared for them so long ago.

Pagan storytellers once claimed the wall between life and death becomes thin this time of year. The church may have been influenced by these stories when it placed the Feast of All Saints on the calendar. I am not sure if this season is truly different or if it is all a trick of the low autumn light, but when I notice a spray of golden leaves at the end of a long country road, it seems to mark a doorway.

I imagine reaching out and brushing aside a narrow curtain of fog. There, just on the edge of this everyday world, is a gathering of the departed and the one who called them on. I, who have felt so alone since coming here, am in the midst of a crowd. They are near, only separated from me by a breath.

I wonder if my life might be different if I were to forget the lies of concrete and fluorescent light. I wonder what might change if I stopped more often to feel the nearness of the past and remember the swiftness of a life span. What if I lived as if a great cloud of witnesses were as close as the sunlight beckoning from the other end of the covered bridge? What if I lived as if each day brought me closer to that light?

These are questions I never asked before coming home to Maplehurst. To consider the nearness of death used to make me feel as if this world didn't matter. Isn't it passing away? But now I begin to see that this world isn't passing away, in the sense of becoming irrelevant. Instead, it is being renewed. The dead are near because this earth still matters. The drama is unfolding here on this dirt. Here beneath this canopy of yellow maple leaves.

I grew up with the word *testimony*. It was a word for dramatic, before-and-after conversions. It was a word for *what is God doing in your life?* It was a word that always made me nervous, as if I were being measured and found wanting. As if the things I cared about—playing in the dollhouse with my best friend or reading a book spread out on the itchy St. Augustine grass of our Texas backyard—did not really matter in the spiritual scheme of things.

I don't think anyone has asked about my testimony in years, which is a shame. Because I have finally figured out something important. Testimony isn't about measuring up. It's about opening our eyes.

What is God doing in my life? In the mornings, I wake to find that he has traced the world in silver. Every blade of grass. Each pumpkin on the porch. In the afternoons, I find him washing these fields with the mellow sunlight of autumn. He has gilded every rail in the fence and the sheet metal roof of the old red barn. He has transformed familiar trees into something otherworldly. They are torches. They are bonfires. They are flames dancing on the edge of my vision.

How do I join God in his work? I lose whole minutes staring at the maple tree outside my window. I can't see the cloud racing past the sun, so I am startled when the tree suddenly catches the light. It was only a tree, but now it is fire from top to bottom.

48

I kneel in the dirt in a cathedral of maple trees. My trowel is almost useless in the bony soil, but I persist. While Lillian holds her baby sister on the porch, I bury 250 bulbs. Their names are prayers: daffodil, tulip, crocus, and scilla. They are papery. They are dusty. Like little more than a bag of onions.

But I am a believer. I know they are like the beautiful souls of those who've gone before. I will see them resurrected in the spring.

Giving Thanks
in Rising Darkness

Enter his gates with thanksgiving and his courts
with praise.

Psalm 100:4

Compared with October, November is somehow both darker and
brighter. The days are shorter and colder. There are only a few
snatches of color left flying raggedly from the trees. Everything
green has washed away. But there is also the promise of the holidays,
a promise of candlelight and shiny silver and the gold rims on the
flutes we raised at our wedding. I always forget about those flutes,
gathering dust in that one small cupboard over the refrigerator
until November circles back to greet us.

Our first Thanksgiving at Maplehurst means more to me than
any single day has a right to mean. It is a container that can't
possibly contain everything I want it to. Trying to say a proper

51

thank-you for my life at Maplehurst is like trying to say thank you for life itself. I simply cannot do it. Or, if I can, it is only by aiming much lower. By narrowing my glance. By believing that even one brief blessing spoken before a meal, while I hold a small hand in each of mine, can be enough.

For so much has changed in one year. I can hardly hold the changes in my mind. Last Thanksgiving, another baby was a dream so far buried I could not even have articulated it to myself. Last Thanksgiving, we ate a pale turkey breast alone with our three children while the air conditioner hummed and rattled down the hall. This year, we have come home. Our family has grown, and we have invited some of our oldest friends to celebrate with us at Maplehurst. Dear friends who now live only two hours away. Giving thanks to God with them will draw a circle around our years.

It is easy to feel gratitude as I place an order for a large turkey with a local Amish farmer. As I discuss the menu with my friend over the phone. It is harder at the edges of the day. In the morning, my body seems heavier. I have to talk myself into leaving my bed. In the evening, I worry. Lists upon lists of things I must not forget begin racing past my eyes as I lie in bed. The long nights of nursing and bottle-feeding and washing and reassembling the plastic pieces of my pump are the explanation I give to a growing dread. Yet the darkness moving through my mind seems untouched by any explanation.

I have always imagined gratitude as a kind of discipline. It is a practice. A choice. I still think this is true. However, I begin to glimpse a long-buried and misguided assumption. I have believed that the practice of noticing good gifts in my life would widen some sort of divine exchange. As if noticing the gifts and giving thanks for them could bring me more of what I noticed.

These days are dark, and I sometimes think I glimpse floodwaters rising. Yet because of November's emphasis on gratitude, I cannot help but lift up my eyes to the mountains (Ps. 121:1). What if gratitude is more about seeing the face of God? Of locking our eyes on his and remembering where our help comes from? Perhaps gratitude is not only a discipline but also a gift, one we are given in special measure just before we pass through the door to suffering.

As dry leaves bury us in drifts like snow, we continue to tread the water of our ever-growing list of home repairs. The promise of houseguests is like a lightning strike. We feel both alarm and a jolt of energy. Every day we walk the gap between our reality of peeling paint and wood floors so worn they give us splinters, and our dreams, such as a picket fence washed in brilliant white. With guests coming to stay, we make a wild effort to bridge the chasm between our days and our dreams. We decide to paint the dining room.

Painting the dining room means painting the walls. It also means painting the frames of the tall wooden windows. It means painting the radiator as well as the water pipes that snake up toward the ceiling. It means painting both the inside and outside of the built-in, glass-fronted cabinets. It means painting three doors and at least the first three steps of the back stairs; after that they curve up and out of sight. It means painting the tall, Victorian baseboards but, most of all, it means painting every slat and beam in the intricate, wooden ceiling.

It is entirely, ridiculously beyond our capacity. With Thanksgiving only a week away, Jonathan paints late at night while I nurse Elsa far from the fumes. While she sleeps, we take turns climbing the ladder and craning our necks. We hope to finish with plenty of time for airing out the drying paint. The last thing I want is to serve our locally pastured turkey with a heavy dose of chemical vapor. We finish with only one day to spare, and that, in itself, is a miracle. We turn on a fan and pray that our high-priced ecological paint will deliver on its promises.

On Thanksgiving Day, the room is entirely new. The dingy pass-through that was our dining room is gone. This room is stunning. I can see now how much beauty lies locked up in our dreams for this place. I can hardly imagine ever picking up a paintbrush again, but I also want to dedicate myself to releasing the potential of this home, room by room.

One week earlier, the walls were a sad shade of beige. It may once have been a lovely color but had faded to look more like an unpleasant stain. Now the walls are an elegant, moody charcoal. Since moving in, we had hardly noticed the beams that lay in rows along the ceiling. Their hand-cut imperfections had disappeared in a sloppy wash of faded white. Now they are picked out in brilliant contrast. Bright white beams against charcoal planks.

Our dishes and glassware had sat invisibly in the built-in cabinets. Now our collection of rose-colored transferware, the entire set bought for twelve dollars at a long-ago garage sale, shines out from the dark colored paint like museum china. The paint is sometimes black, sometimes dark gray and, when the sun shines in, sometimes a perfect navy blue.

This is the first truly beautiful thing we have given this house, and we've finished it just in time for Thanksgiving. I am relieved, thankful even, but I also know the effort has nearly wiped us out. Everything is harder than I anticipated. Each task requires more, and there are more of them than I ever imagined. Too often my mood, my whole outlook, matches the new color of this room. It is the color of storm clouds as they move in your direction.

For a moment, I submit to the storm. I listen to what the darkness in my head is saying. That it is futile. Why bother? The paint will fade and chip. Our friends probably won't even notice what we've done to the room. The money for pricy low-vapor paint should have been given to the poor. We are foolish to lavish any of our love on a crumbling house.

I finally halt in my train of thought only because I cannot think my way past so many dead ends. That is when I hear a different voice. A sweetly familiar voice. *This room will look beautiful by candlelight.*

This house is deteriorating. My body is dying. We are subject to the same terrible decay. But worth is not measured in such terms. Once upon a time, God called his creation good. And no curse of sin unwound those words. Gnarled maple trees. Plaster walls. An ordinary woman's ordinary body. All good. To care for these is to say to death, "You are not the end."

Because I share the ancient Christian hope of resurrection, I believe that the goodness of creation will endure. And not only will it endure, but it will also be renewed. Will an old house like Maplehurst persist, in some new way, on a remade earth? I don't know. But I believe Thanksgiving prayers and memories of special meals have what it takes to pass through the flames. They, too, are a part of a creation that is good. Surely we will hear their echo, taste it even, at that last great wedding feast.

And, oh, how we feast. Our turkey is crisp and brown. Soft, golden potato rolls made from my mother's recipe pair perfectly with spicy apple butter. The Brussels sprouts are sweetly caramelized. The children are quiet in their seats, rendered speechless by buttery peaks of mashed potatoes. Between first servings and seconds, we pass around a small wooden bowl filled with popcorn kernels. For each kernel we take we offer up some gratitude. Today in this beautiful room, with good friends and good food, it is easy to do. We pass the bowl again and again and again.

We have been promised a day when God will restore everything (Acts 3:21). I do not think it is too much to hope that one thing I will gather up on that day is a memory of our first meal in this room. How our conversation deepens as the sun sets and the moon

55

comes out. How the dimmed lights of the chandelier's bulbs shine like stars against the ceiling's dark sky. Of the way the candlelight moves in Jonathan's eyes as he tells the story of our coming home.

I will remember how it is only in darkness that I can see how bright are the white beams above our heads. And I will never forget how beautiful a gold-rimmed glass can be when it is held by the hands that are more familiar to me than even my own. Hands washed with dots of paint. White paint and charcoal, like a constellation of all the dreams we have shared.

Set Apart

Who may ascend the mountain of the LORD? Who
may stand in his holy place?

Psalm 24:3

My older children return to school as the last days of November
spin themselves out in a fog. Maplehurst is tucked into the foothills
that lie halfway between the Atlantic Ocean and the Pennsylvania
mountains. In winter, we are ruled by the cold, dry mountain air,
but the warmth and humidity of the sea retreat slowly, churning
up a great deal of fog as they go.

I sit in the tufted armchair by the parlor window holding Elsa,
and I strain to follow two overstuffed backpacks the whole way
from the front porch to the street. Inevitably, they dissolve, fading
into the general grayness well before they reach their bus stop.

Each morning while I search the fog for the glow of school bus
headlights, I witness the progress of a startling transformation. As
the last of the leaves spin in dizzy circles to the ground, Maplehurst
loses its green isolation. The split-rail fences, buried by wild grape
vines in summer and fall, begin to reveal their skeletal structure.

Twining hedgerows are replaced by faded fences wrapped in bony twigs. Damaged rails that had been hidden now stand out like broken teeth.

For the first time since moving here, I am confronted by the new houses that ring us in. I never realized just how near they are. Maplehurst is exposed, and I begin to feel as if the trees have betrayed us. They seem to flaunt their naked branches against the sky. The view appears bare and lifeless even when I study it through the carnival glass of my bedroom windows.

Something significant happened to our world because Jesus walked here, because he died here and lived again here. While God had always met with people in sacred places—like mountaintops or the temple—Jesus cracked open that familiar mold. Since Jesus, *every place* has the potential to be sacred. We carry God with us now; our bodies are temples.

But if the temple doors have been thrown open and the whole world has become the setting for God's encounters with us, then do particular places matter any longer? If all space is sacred, then is any place special? I had thought Maplehurst unique. I had seen it as set apart, though for what, I hardly knew. Now I am less sure.

Certainly the momentum in our day is to erase the uniqueness of unique places. Rocky foothills and prairie grasslands look much the same beneath a smooth coating of concrete. The sidewalks and cul-de-sacs of my new neighborhood are difficult to distinguish from the sidewalks and cul-de-sacs of my old neighborhood.

It is the same with time. The floodlights that illuminate our parking lots also flatten out the difference between night and day. It is only in the wake of some catastrophe, small like a power outage or large like a night spent with your child in the hospital, that we notice the gradations between one second and the next. In our age, remaining attuned to the distinction between one place and another, between one day and another, seems to require an act of ferocious strength.

It is like trying to return to the beginning. To those glory days when God first brought harmony out of chaos. In the beginning, he separated land and sea. In this way, he created the distinctiveness of the earth's many places. In the beginning, he separated day and night. He also distinguished the sixth day from the seventh. In these ways, God created the ordered space humans would need to flourish.

I fear we override these natural limits to our peril. Thanks to technology, work bleeds into every moment of our lives. There is always the temptation to do more. To be more productive. To live with more efficiency. It is a terrible burden to bear. For us, as well as the earth beneath our feet.

I believe in sacred time. We may live in a world of Sunday-morning soccer games, Sunday-afternoon birthday parties, and twenty-four-hour shopping, but I believe there are days when eternity floods our time-bound existence. Days like a cup that runneth over. I also know that without some effort on my part, all time tends to look exactly the same, whether or not it is the same.

Advent is beginning, and I want to set aside the days. To mark them off and probe their depths. I want this for myself, and I want it for my children. But I have no strength. I feel too tired. Too fretful. Too overwhelmed. At Maplehurst, Advent is the darkest time of the year. But darkness isn't only a condition on the other side of your window.

Sometimes it is a heaviness in your chest. Sometimes it is a fog behind your eyes. Sometimes it is a creeping sickness caused by . . . shifting hormones? Sleep deprivation? I don't know, but I am beginning to accept that neither these thick brick walls, nor even the heavy, velvet curtains I've hung over our parlor windows can keep it out.

My Advent observance took on new meaning in the dark days of my wilderness wandering. I was desperate for light and newness, and though I believed my own efforts couldn't make the light dawn any sooner, I wanted to be ready when it did. I wanted to be there, waiting, with eyes wide open for those first streaks of gold in the eastern sky. This year I hold the gift of Elsa in my arms. I rock her to sleep in my dream home, but there is a darkness growing in my mind. A fog I cannot seem to escape.

Fog is insubstantial. A mere vapor. Only a mist. Yet it has the power to remake our whole world. Paths disappear in it; obstacles like tree roots and boulders are absorbed by it, then released the moment we come near. Fog is the sky, fallen all around us. Only a fool begins a journey in the fog. Yet what choice do I have?

Here is the paradox of Advent: it is a journey through a season of quiet preparation, but this is quietness like tremors before an earthquake. Every day is moving us closer to momentous change: the anniversary of a baby's birth, the second coming of a King. Yes, it is misty and dark. All seems still and unchanging. Lifeless and barren. But if we pay attention, we can feel the world turning. We can feel the whole globe rushing beneath our planted feet.

Stand still long enough, and you will feel each day turning. You will feel even yourself turning. At Advent, we come back to the beginning (a new church year and a baby's birth), but we are also closer to the end (a wedding supper and a kingdom fully come). Like the movement of our planet, sometimes the swiftest path forward is also a return.

Perhaps every place has the potential to be sacred space, but I cannot meet with God in every place. I am one woman. I am married, and I care for young children. I am tied to this particular plot of ground by responsibility and by love. Yet not even Adam and Eve were given the world. They were given each other. They were given one garden, as I have been given one garden.

It has been a long time since the exile from Eden. I do not know, but I long to know, if God still walks with us here.

WINTER

The Sound of a Silent Voice

"Shout and be glad, Daughter Zion. For I am coming,
and I will live among you," declares the LORD.

Zechariah 2:10

The calendar tacked to the kitchen wall reads December. The
church calendar in my head says Advent. No matter which name
I give it, this is a month for waiting. We are waiting for Christmas
and remembering the world's long wait for the Redeemer. But to
me, both appear too distant. Too abstract. I long for something
real. Something I can see with my eyes and feel on my skin.

The only thing I am waiting for is snow.

I have been waiting a long time. Almost three years ago, Jonathan and I moved to a place without winter weather. We arrived
with heavy coats draped over our arms. The box holding our boots
was wrinkled and soft where melting snow had left its mark. If I
had known what the next few years would be like, I would have
wept over that soggy cardboard. But we do not always recognize

the wilderness when we first cross its borders. I could not have guessed a place of warm breezes and rustling palms was to be the setting for a two-year winter of the soul.

Now I am sure my long winter in the wilderness has ended. In September, we named our daughter Elsa Spring. Her name had nothing to do with the calendar page on the wall and everything to do with the words I remembered when I held her for the first time: "Behold, the winter is past; the rain is over and gone. The flowers appear on the earth, the time of singing has come" (Song 2:11–12 ESV). Yet today, through the dim northern window of Elsa's nursery, I can see only mud, bare trees, and split-rail fences choked with the bony fingers of dead, gray vines.

I believe that winter of the soul has passed, but I believe against all the evidence of my body, even the view through this window. I can no longer remember why I should bother to get out of bed. I am no longer sure why it matters if I wash the breakfast dishes or not. I feel drained of every emotion except the anxiety left rattling around in the dry husk of my self.

I long for a world made new by snow. I long for snowflakes to flutter past the window the way blossoms from an apple tree scatter on a spring breeze. I want snow so badly I ache. I want to be tucked in beneath still, beautiful whiteness. I want to sleep on and on. Some corner of my mind knows that I should ask for help. That I should see a doctor. Instead, weighed down by emptiness, I do nothing but keep my eyes lifted toward the clouds.

The baby girl I prayed for is not even three months old, we have lived in the farmhouse of our dreams only a few weeks longer than that, but I have reached the end of myself. It turned out to be a very short journey, and I am ashamed that this is so. God parted the waters and brought me to the promised land, and I return the favor by snapping at my children and fretting over the unseasonably warm weather. Instead of doing my part, I fill the beautiful white porcelain sink in the kitchen with dirty dishes and leave them there.

I am overwhelmed by all that has been given to me, yet I seem to need more. Though I have prayed for months that God would allow me to nurse my daughter, I have heard no response. Worse, the unresolved turmoil of my hormones seems to have unleashed some darkness in my mind. I have stopped praying for more milk for my baby and now pray only this: *don't leave me in this terrible, empty place.*

I hear nothing. The words in my Bible are flat. There is no comforting whisper. I wonder if I have done something wrong. I wonder if God is teaching me some lesson. Have I been too focused on the gifts of God's hands and neglected to look for his face? Is that why I can no longer hear his voice?

Through the fog of my anxiety, I discern one small glimmer of grace. God has given me a home, a place to which I feel sure I belong. My wandering days have ended, and I know the road to happiness and wholeness will not be found in some other place. I rest in the knowledge that I will find these things at Maplehurst—or find them not at all.

I can hear the silver sound of rain falling on the metal roof of the small red barn, but I am straining my ears for quiet. When rain turns to snow, silence heralds its advent. I remember the many silent years between the words God speaks in the book of Malachi and the Word whose birth is announced in the book of Matthew. I imagine God's chosen people lifting cries for help to the heavens and receiving only silence in return. But I encounter this centuries-long gap on the other side of Christ's coming. From this vantage, it seems clear that God had not removed himself. He was not waiting for his people to learn their lesson. Silence was no punishment.

When something breaks down or does not go as planned, we are given a glimpse of our great need. Like a vast emptiness. We pray for solutions, crying out for immediate help, but God desires to give us more. To give something real. Something we can see with our eyes and feel on our skin. Like a baby born to us.

But first he fills that emptiness with his silence. And we, tuning our ears to it, are made ready to recognize his answer. We are made ready to recognize him. I imagine the silence building and building over centuries until those who strained their ears, like Simeon and Anna in the temple, could hear the silence speak: "I am coming. Hold on. I am coming."

Let There Be Light

Sing for joy, you heavens.

Isaiah 44:23

In December, the neighborhood around Maplehurst is stricken with another kind of silence. During the fall, I had sometimes caught the sounds of children playing and neighbors laughing. I could not see beyond the ring of trees and shrubs and runaway vines, but those sounds were like a promise. They told me my isolation was only temporary. Occasionally I would even send Thaddeus or Lillian scouting between the bushes. *Go see if you can make a friend.* It never worked. We never could catch the sounds that teased us from beyond green walls. Echoes were all we had.

In the raw wind and rain of early December, even the echoes are lost to me. I know people live in these houses. I can see lights in windows. I sometimes catch a glimpse of a garage door closing silently. But without snow to draw the children out on sleds, our neighborhood feels empty and deserted. Surrounded, we are alone.

We gather in our dining room after dinner, the two tall windows mirrors of darkness. The small candle bulbs in the old chandelier cast more shadows than light. The newly painted walls are a soft black, as if the evening sky has pressed itself all the way down and into this room. It is only after the children's usual tussle over the box of matches that I can see, by the light of the first candle, the familiar beauty of our Advent wreath.

I found the wreath years ago at a German Christmas market. It is handmade of pale wood. Four wooden arms hold four brass candleholders, and four wooden angels hold small wooden trumpets to their lips. A wooden star rises from the center. The wood is unstained and simply varnished, but the star and the trumpets and the wings on the angels are picked out in soft gold paint.

This year my precious wreath seems smaller, lost in the dark, empty space between the tabletop and the faraway ceiling. The dim, golden star offers no light. And what good are tiny wooden trumpets if they are silent? They cannot compete with the bickering of my children.

Lillian asks why we light the candles each night, and I respond automatically, "To remember the wait for Jesus." That word *remember* suddenly seems so inadequate. If remembering is just the shift of thoughts in my head (oh, yes, I need to buy milk, or oh, yes, God was born to us), then Advent hardly matters at all. I need more. I need a star bright enough to chase away the darkness. I need a trumpet blast loud enough to penetrate the silence of these lonely winter days.

I have often heard followers of Jesus explain dark times with talk of the *now* and the *not yet* of the kingdom of God. That kingdom inaugurated on earth in the muck of a stable bathed in starlight. Our *now* is the victory over death Jesus achieved in an empty tomb. Yet this world still rocks with wars and rumors of wars. This world is still held in the strong grip of decay. Sin and death and all their attendants, from depression to famine, still have the power to make us weep. That, they say, reveals the vast extent of heaven's *not yet*.

The *now* and the *not yet* is a theological truth too often reduced to a platitude. We speak these words and intend comfort, but when I think of them, I feel only despair. My now is dark and silent, and if the way of the world has been reordered, if the power of death has been broken, I struggle to see it.

Maplehurst is *now*, and it is *not yet*, but I find that tension unbearable. Our now is a neighborhood of strangers and a large rectangle of weedy grass where we hope a vegetable garden can grow. *Not yet* is an early spring planting of lettuces and peas in raised beds secured by a pretty picket fence. We should have begun weeks ago to smother the matted sod with cardboard and compost. I worry that it is now too late.

Earlier today, a dump truck finally unloaded a mountain of mushroom compost near the site of our hoped-for garden. Mushroom compost, a by-product of the mushroom farms that dominate our local economy, sounds lovely and vegetarian, but it is a noxious mess of horse manure. I watched the steam rise from that pile, I choked on the stench of it, and I felt no relief at all. *Now* is my anxious depression. *Now* is a tyrannical to-do list that offers no satisfaction when I check something off. *Not yet* is far away, so far even hope cannot reach it.

I was a child when I first learned to say, "This is the day the LORD has made; We will rejoice and be glad in it" (Ps. 118:24 NKJV). Back then these words were sweet and easy. I hadn't yet experienced the heavy burden of yesterdays and tomorrows. I hadn't yet discovered how that burden makes it so difficult to feel at home in our today.

This may be why I struggle against the idea of the *now* and the *not yet*. We only think in these terms when we are dissatisfied with our *now*. When we are overrun by trouble. On those days, we remind ourselves that the kingdom to which we have pledged our lives is not yet fully arrived. And then we sit back, chastened. We are stuck in an imperfect reality we do not, in ourselves, have the power to change. The *not yet* no longer seems to be good news. It seems to taunt us, to tease us, to say what we have is not good enough. If we are always comparing our *now* with our *not yet*, then we will find it impossible to be glad in the day that God has given.

What might happen if I loosen my grip on the perfection of the *not yet*? What if I stop acting as if *not yet* is something I can achieve? Something I am supposed to muscle into existence? I want to learn to live in today as I live in this house.

Maplehurst is far from perfect. As old as it is, it remains unfinished. I know this every time I discover a new water stain on the slope of the third-floor ceiling. Or every time I trip over the broken floorboard on the porch. The time for those repairs will come. But today is a day for chatting with the local man who gave us such a good deal on the compost. He promised there was nothing better for growing vegetables. Today is a day for unpacking our favorite Christmas books and stacking them in tottering piles on the deep sills of the parlor windows. Today is a day for lighting candles.

If I light these candles to remember the long-ago wait for Jesus, then I want my remembering to look like God's remembering. God remembered Noah, and it took the form of a wind. God remembered Hannah, and it took the form of a son. This kind of remembering is so powerful it joins the *now* and the *not yet*.

When Jesus broke the bread and served the wine, he said, "Do this in remembrance of me" (Luke 22:19). *Do this.* He didn't say "think this" or "keep retrieving this idea from the back of your brain." He didn't even say "feel this." No. He said, "Do this." Jesus knew the day of his coming was a long one. Thousands of years after his birth, we are still living in it. Of course we would grow tired on this long day. Of course we would begin to wonder if the old stories have lost their power. So God gave us a command: "do this." *Eat this and drink this and remember me.*

———

Advent embodies the *now* and the *not yet*. But the *now* of Advent is a spacious place. A pleasant place. I am given good things to do, things that are not at all burdensome. I must eat. I must drink. I must sleep. I must cut branches from the holly tree and bring them indoors. I must not rush my children into bed before I have sat with them and held their hands and said one prayer to the accompaniment of tiny angels with quiet, golden horns.

If I want to abide in this day, to make my home in it, I must only tear my eyes from tomorrow and look around. For there is a wholeness to this day that I do not want to miss. As established in the beginning, there is evening and morning. There is sun and moon. There is the cacophony of daytime living and the quiet music of nighttime rest.

Even if darkness remains and the winter nights are long, when else can I appreciate the beauty of all the little lights? The candles in our wreath. The lamplight glowing from behind my neighbor's curtain. Certainly, I can sometimes find a daytime moon, but it is a pale, faded thing. Only a nighttime moon washes the world in watery light. And this year, something new. Without fully understanding the tradition, we have followed the example set by every other old farmhouse in our town. We have placed electric candles in each of our front windows.

As I walk back from the mailbox in the dark just after the children's bedtime, I keep my eyes on the six lights that twinkle just ahead. They are small, but this only serves to concentrate their brightness. Here, so far from a city, the cloudless night sky is always swirled with stars. This night, it looks as if six of them have come to live with us. It is so still out here after dark that I almost imagine I can hear their song. It is a quiet song. It is a nighttime song. One more good gift of today.

A Good and Terrible Story

Lift up your heads, you gates; be lifted up, you ancient doors, that the King of glory may come in.

Psalm 24:7

In this house, I am always stumbling over the past. I find it, especially, as I move along the ragged edges of this place, like the narrow enclosure of the back stairs. Many steps over many years have worn a smooth depression on each pine tread. They fit my foot exactly. I often climb those stairs with my mind holding tightly to some task like a balloon on a string. When my foot falls into a hollow, I lose my grip on the balloon. I lose touch with the house today, and I drop down into the deep well of the home's long past.

How many feet, how many lives, does it take to leave such an impression in wood? This house was built in 1880. Casting my mind so far back, I register the bumps and ridges of history-making days, but I wonder most about the unremembered sorrow. The private grief. I sometimes imagine I can still hear the distant sounds of a young maid crying herself to sleep in one of the attic bedrooms.

Old houses hold their stories in worn wood and chimneys that no longer correspond to any fireplace. They reveal their secrets in newsprint found tucked within the lath and plaster walls. In square-headed nails and handworked moldings. Some days I imagine the many happy tales, the stories of births and marriages and good harvests. But there are days when I cannot escape the sound of weeping. Did God keep watch over those who cried?

The psalmist tells us that God has listed our tears in his scroll (Ps. 56:8). In Maplehurst, I have been given a glimpse of that record.

One December morning, I sent my older son to school crying. Jonathan was traveling for work, and I was left to nurse Elsa, prepare breakfast for myself and three kids, make two school lunches, and oversee the dressing of squirmy bodies and the brushing of loose teeth. By 7:20 in the morning. Of course, we began to run late. Of course, my voice became more shrill. My eyes more than a little wild.

Thaddeus has a dreamer's tendency to lose homework and mittens. When he told me he could not find his shoes, I did all the things mothers know not to do, and I watched myself do them. But the worst were the words themselves, the words I yelled at a little boy with freckles on his nose. *What is wrong with you?*

If it had been any other day, I would have pulled myself together soon after his school bus arrived. I would have planned my afternoon apology and gone on with my day. But not long after my first-grader climbed the steps to his bus, his face a mess of freckles and tears, something terrible happened in a first-grade classroom at Sandy Hook Elementary School. This same afternoon, not so very far away, there would be empty seats on school buses. There would be mothers and fathers who would never again say, "I'm sorry. I love you."

I never did pull myself together. I dropped tears on Elsa's cheeks while she nursed. I dropped more tears on the Candyland board game. Unaware of what had happened but sensing my preoccupation, Beau set up the game again and again and again. Perhaps unwilling to push his luck, he never complained about tears muddling all the happy, candy colors.

It is the following Sunday when Thaddeus decides we must have an impromptu nativity play in the family room. The winter sun is low in the sky, and the light fills the tall west-facing windows of this room. With the sun warming our sweaters, we can almost forget how much the temperature had dropped in recent days. With the sun in our eyes, we cannot see the stockade fence that stands between these windows and the houses nearest our own on this side of the hill. Our world is safely contained within the four plaster walls of one room.

Thaddeus narrates from his rocking horse "camel," and Lillian sits slumped in her angel costume, her scowl at odds with the gold glitter of her wings. I realize that my children have never been told the full story. Our illustrated children's Bible doesn't mention the murder of the innocents. I suppose this is because they *are* the innocents. We sanitize their Bibles. We keep the radio and television news turned off when they are in the room. I choke back my tears, because I don't want them to know how bad it is. How dark and terrible this world truly is. I don't want them to hear this:

> A voice is heard in Ramah,
>> weeping and great mourning,
> Rachel weeping for her children
>> and refusing to be comforted,
>> because they are no more. (Matt. 2:18)

My children already love Advent and Christmas. They love it enough to act out the story, to offer a basket of dominoes in place of gold. They love it, though they have not yet heard the whole narrative.

One day they will know just how good and just how terrible the story is. They will know what Rachel's voice sounds like, and they won't be able to rid their minds and hearts of its awful cadence.

I cannot spare them forever. Always there are more heartbroken mothers. Always there are more tears. But they will also know Emmanuel. They will know the good news of incarnation. That God walks with them, always *already* in the darkest places. He is especially present in the very places we imagine he cannot be. He is there holding Rachel, whispering his promises. *It will not always be like this.*

I never really noticed the stockade fence until Jonathan mentioned it. During the warmer months, it was hidden behind a green screen. Even now that the green has died away, I have somehow managed not to see the solid fence that separates Maplehurst from the houses nearest to the western edge of our hill. Jonathan says he thinks we should tear it down and reveal the split-rail fence that continues in its loop behind it. He wonders if we shouldn't give our neighbors something nicer to look at than the faded backside of a prefabricated fence. He imagines children might one day run back and forth between these yards.

But I want to hide. I want to keep our kids safe and near. I want to fence them in as securely as I can. I say only "let's see." Later, as I stand at the kitchen sink, I catch sight of Jonathan out by that fence, giving it a shake and trying to test the strength of its foundation. Speculating how hard it would be to hammer it down.

Me, I want to hide from the horror out there. I want only to sing of drifting snow and silent nights, but I am walking an Advent road, and I can't easily forget that Mary sang of justice not silence. I suppose Mary's is the first Advent hymn. Or the first Christmas carol. In it the proud are scattered. The rich sent away empty. It is the humble and the hungry who receive.

Jesus welcomed children and wept at tombs and showed us what the kingdom of God is like. In his kingdom, love lays down its right to safety. To privacy. This love is willing to be inconvenienced and interrupted. This love seeks justice for the weak and the small and redeems even the most despised. This love loves neighbor as it loves itself.

Part of me still wants the oblivion of snow. But grief has rattled the bars of my empty, anxious self, and I know now that I also want something else. I want a hammer. It is time to tear down our fences. It is time to open our gates.

Starlight and Dust

Praise him, sun and moon; praise him, all you
shining stars.

Psalm 148:3

This morning I turned on the faucet at the kitchen sink but was
greeted only by a slow drizzle. I thought there must be something wrong with the water pressure, but then the water stopped
altogether. I stood with my red electric kettle in one hand and
puzzled over what to do. I couldn't quite face the possibility that
there would be no French press coffee and, maybe, not even an
afternoon cup of Darjeeling tea.

Maplehurst is not connected to the municipal water system that
supplies the surrounding neighborhood. We have a well, dug fairly
recently and deeply by the previous owners after the old original
well dried up. I stood at the sink and remembered their story of
the day the well ran dry, and I began to worry.

Later I would wonder if it was the lack of caffeine that had
made me so vulnerable to his throwaway comment. Perhaps it
was my anxiety about the well. Maybe I would have felt it keenly

regardless. What I know is that when the well repairman stood at my kitchen window and said, "It's such a shame," I felt my face flush with embarrassment, then anger.

His hair was more gray than brown. He had lived in the area all of his life and knew what the view from my window once must have been. A rolling, patchwork view of pastureland and cropland reaching out and up to the distant hills. The view was still there. It still drew our eyes down and out across the lowland and up again toward those far hills, but now it was a rolling stretch of faded lawns dotted with identical vinyl-wrapped homes. It was "a shame," he said.

The well repairman determined it was only an electrical problem in the pump. He assured us we need never worry that our extra-deep well will run dry. Now as I prepare dinner I am more aware of the gift of running water, but I am also aware of the tender spot where his words have lodged.

I do not know my neighbors, but I feel compelled to defend them. To say, yes, I too love a pristine view, but there is also something beautiful about backyard grills and trampolines and swing sets. There is something beautiful about people living their ordinary lives side by side. But is there something *too* strident about my inner protest? I feel this man's words crack open my own repository of doubt. Secret doubts I have never acknowledged murmur, like this saucepan of water just coming to a boil.

Perhaps a farmhouse without a farm is not a special place. Maybe it is a compromised place. Perhaps the view from my kitchen window isn't beautiful but spoiled. I remember, too, that Jonathan found a mystery puddle in the basement this week. And this is mushroom farming country—there are so many days I can hardly breathe for the stench of manure in the air.

Even Elsa Spring. I smile just to think of her upstairs taking an early evening nap. She has been a good, a perfect gift. But with her birth have come panic and tears, panic and tears. I no longer think about recovery. Only moment-by-moment survival.

So many dreams are coming true, but it is as if they are being realized in dust and dirt and darkness. Some part of me still knows the bigger story. It begins in a stable but ends with streets of gold. I know this. I know it well. But there are no streets of gold in my neighborhood. There is endless asphalt and dogs barking too loudly and too late. There is no neighborhood park or gathering place, but there are playsets in every individual backyard. In my own yard, there is a steaming heap of horse manure like an insulting placeholder for the garden of my dreams.

I moved from palm trees to maple trees on a tidal wave of gratitude. But now, as the days contract, I can feel gratitude slipping through my fingers. Every good gift from recent months seems to have its tarnished edge. I realize that all along, without even noticing what I do, I have been mentally sifting good from bad. I have been sorting out blessing from burden. I suddenly feel too tired to keep it up. My gratitude is clouded with misgivings, and I no longer have the strength to strain them out.

After dinner, we go for a walk. It is the day's Advent activity: take a walk in the neighborhood to see Christmas lights! That is what was written on the little note the kids found stuffed in mitten number twenty of the Advent garland. And so we stuff ourselves, like six marshmallows, into our coats and hats, and pass single file through the gap in the split-rail fence. We walk past the cave that was once a smokehouse. We walk past the crumbling roots of the old stone barn. Once there, we point our toes down until we land on the sidewalk.

The moment our boots touch smooth cement, we are in a different world. This is an ordinary suburban world. A world of vinyl siding, tidy yards, newly planted trees, and inflatable Christmas creatures. Advent has always meant wonder to me, and I suppose to chase wonder is to find yourself in unexpected places. Like a line at the post office. Or the LEGO store at the shopping mall. Or, perhaps, even the quiet streets of the suburban-style neighborhood that spread out just beyond our line of trees.

We may not depict these ordinary places on Christmas cards. We may not celebrate them in song. But this is where we live, and wonder lives here too. The wise men would understand. They imagined the star would lead them to a palace.

Tonight, the stars above are cold and brilliant. The lights below are vivid and multicolored. They somehow manage to appear both ridiculous and wonderful. The children exclaim over both, the lights above and the lights below, without discernment. And why not? We walk every day on a spinning planet, a bright beacon, a blue-and-green jewel. Stunning miracles are our daily bread.

Dazzled by these lights, I realize that I am finished with sifting. Finished trying to untangle the knots of good and bad. Finished naming one thing a gift, another a curse. I am finished with sorting out the sacred from the everyday. I am dreaming of a garden, but I understand that I can't have it without that wretched mountain of manure. I can't have Maplehurst, the house, without the neighborhood in which it now sits. These things must be embraced entirely or not embraced at all.

Advent pours itself into Christmas, and I must embrace both. They are two parts of a whole. I love the anticipation of Advent. I love the expectation. Christmas always leaves me feeling more than a bit let down. Of course, it is better now that I'm grown. Christmas doesn't end the evening of December 25. We do our best to celebrate the season. But with my anticipation strengthening over so many Advent days, disappointment often seems inevitable.

I become so focused on waiting that I forget what I am waiting for is mostly already here. Not entirely, but every year Christ's kingdom is more established. Perhaps, what I wait for during Advent is not the coming of Jesus but eyes open more widely to the fact that he is always and already with us—in so many everyday ways. This season is both extraordinary (wintry starlight and Beethoven's "Ode to Joy") and beautifully ordinary (meals cooked and shared, phone calls made and received). It is starlight and dust.

I, too, am dust, but I breathe with God's own breath, don't I? This night, walking in the frosty air, I use that breath to say thank you. Thank you for all of it. The compost in my yard and the dishes in the sink. I cry thank you because our God has never despised the dirt, and he once wrapped himself in dust. He is our God with dirt under his nails, and he is near. God with us.

With lights above and lights below, I raise my hands to hold it all. A star is dancing in the baby's eyes, and I follow it onward.

I follow it home.

This Day Runneth Over

And God said, "Let there be lights in the vault of the
sky to separate the day from the night, and let them
serve as signs to mark sacred times, and days, and
years."

Genesis 1:14

The natural world does not generally support our sense of being
the center of the universe. The sky remains blue though our mood
is foul. We wake with enthusiasm only to discover a driving rain.
Clouds obscure the full moon on our special night. I have decided
this only makes the exceptions sweeter. I try not to take the weather
personally, but there are days when that is the only reasonable
thing to do.

We witness our first snowfall at Maplehurst late in the afternoon
on Christmas Eve. The sun has set, but there is just enough light
left hanging in the air to make each snowflake glow. As we tumble
outside and lift our faces to the sky, it is as if one thousand lanterns
are slowly descending to light the Christ child's way.

Snow continues to fall, quietly and lightly, as darkness settles in and Christmas Day approaches. This is no storm. It is a gentle answer, and it needs all night to leave its message on the red-brick chimneys, the steeply sloped roof, each frozen blade of grass, and every bare branch. It is all around us when we wake on Christmas morning. "Come, Lord Jesus," we prayed. "I have come," he answers us.

Seasons are cycles of anticipation and fulfillment. Throughout December we drank deeply of anticipation. We decorated slowly. First, with our Advent wreath and branches from the holly tree near the fence. Later, about a week before Christmas, we cut down a Douglas fir at the tree farm on the edge of town. We trimmed our tree with beautiful memories, including a seashell ornament from our last home and a small glass skyscraper from the home before that. This year we added a silver rocking horse engraved with the words "Baby's First Christmas."

My children are growing up and slipping away. My sisters and I trade texts across three time zones wondering what exactly to do about all these gray hairs, yet in a moment as simple as the unpacking of familiar ornaments, I feel myself held by some stillness deep within the ebb and flow of time. Every season arrives and returns again like the ocean breathing its waves in and out on the shore.

During Advent, we prepare room in a new day for an old story. Through our attentive waiting, we participate in the story of the season and make it new again. And we are made new by it. We emerge at the other end of Advent's tunnel, and we are not as we were when our journey began.

I had waited for snow for such a long time, and I sometimes wondered if there was any point to my hopeful watching. If the end result will be the same because snow will come when snow will come, then why not pass the time thinking of other things?

Why not try to forget that I have new sleds hidden in the basement? It hurts to wait, especially when we do not know how long our wait will last.

How long, Lord, how long? We repeat this ancient cry, and the words echo with all the burdens of a waiting world. Snow, spring, babies, degrees, jobs, weddings, healing, peace, and love. Always, there is something to wait for. I have waited for these and other things, and I have learned that waiting is like wind. It appears to be nothing, but it is a nothing as shapeless yet vital as breath. Waiting molds us, changes us, makes us ready in some way that is hard to grasp. Snow is snow, but snow we have waited for, snow we have longed for, snow we have watched for . . . that is snow as it was always meant to be. It is more itself because *we* have changed. We now have eyes to see and arms open more widely to receive.

What do we receive on the other side of Advent? Christmas Day ushers in fulfillment, and time flows in strange ways. It begins with cinnamon rolls in the pale darkness of early morning. We empty stockings in a few frenzied minutes, but we linger over beef bourguignon at noon. We solve our familiar Christmas village jigsaw puzzle over a few slow hours, and it is the longest afternoon we've ever known. Because of Advent, we are given a day like a cup that runneth over. A day that holds more than twenty-four hours usually can. A day that tastes like eternity.

We watch from the windows as the children play in snow for the first time in years, and we marvel at the strangeness of our familiar yard. The snow has brought a new spaciousness to our hilltop. Corners that had been hidden beneath wild brambles now join the lawn beneath a seamless wash of white. Everything is bigger. Brighter. Made new.

Snow softens edges, but it also reveals them. Jonathan and I can see, for the first time, what it might look like someday when we have cleared all the tangled, overgrown edges of the property. The snow isn't only an answer to my prayer or the fulfillment of my sometimes eager, sometimes weary waiting. It also reveals new possibilities and ushers in the beginning of another cycle of anticipation. This snow-covered yard is like a blank page inviting us to make plans for the garden and urging us on toward the next season's work of clearing and trimming and planting.

This Christmas Day feels as spacious as our snowy hilltop, but like even ordinary days, it does not last forever. As the afternoon light begins to fade, I remember the almost unbearable sadness I always felt as a child at the close of Christmas Day. Back then, I could not bear the thought that I must wait a whole year to experience Christmas joy again. But I understand now that Christmas Day does not mark an end, and I am determined not to treat it as one. There is wisdom in those traditional twelve days. One joy-filled day isn't enough when we have waited for so long.

When the daylight passes its golden moment and begins to gray around the edges, I whisper to Jonathan, "It's time."

Jonathan gathers our secondhand nativity set from the storage box in the basement and slips out the door with the stable and figures tucked under his arm. He carries candles and jam jars in every pocket.

I wrap everyone in coats and slip on their boots. I zip Elsa into the cherry red bunting I purchased a decade ago for her sister; the same bunting each of my babies wore during their first winters. With Elsa strapped securely to my chest, I hand out glass-paned lanterns, each with a flickering tealight candle. After a few warnings about fire safety, we file out the door and begin to walk. Our little lights fade in the general brightness of moonlight on snow.

"Where are we going? What are we doing?"

"We are looking for him," I say.

Lillian is the first to notice a far-off light. "What is that over there?" We follow her pointing finger. By now our footprints circle the house. Dark pools sunk in luminous snow. As we approach the hollow maple tree near the back fence, we notice flickering lights. Our own lantern lights move to greet them until we find, tucked into the base of the tree and just above the collapsed stones of the old barn's foundation, the one we have been seeking all these many days. A baby and a King.

Our wooden crèche sits half buried in snow. Candles in jam jars illuminate our own little Bethlehem. The children forget their cold toes and familiar squabbles. Frosty breath hangs in the air before wide-opened eyes. Someone points out a star overhead, and we all agree that, yes, it does seem extra bright. Yes, it does seem to rest exactly above this spot.

Eventually, we hold hands and sing "Silent Night." We listen to the notes still floating in the cold night air as we follow our footsteps home. Christmas has come. Our King has come.

"Christmas isn't over, is it?" Lillian whispers.

"No," I answer. "This is only the beginning."

How to Cultivate a Year

Build houses and settle down; plant gardens and eat
what they produce.

Jeremiah 29:5

Beau is too young to have any memory of snow, but Lillian and
Thaddeus convince him that the waterproof overalls and clunky
boots are worthwhile. Together, they devote their Christmas vacation to their new sleds, to a crowd of snowmen, and to the subtle
skill required to leave the wingprints of an angel right in our own
front yard. With no effort at all, they remember that even five
minutes in the snow entitles a pink-cheeked child to another mug
of hot chocolate. Beau doesn't need that lesson explained twice.

I pull our old beach towels from a dark cupboard and use them
to mop up puddles of melting snow. Late in the morning, as I have
every morning this week, I begin slowly and deliberately measuring
cloves, allspice, peppercorns, cinnamon, cardamom, and star anise.
My goal is always the same: two steaming cups of sweet, milky
chai. I experiment with tea bags and loose leaf tea and discover
that leafy Ceylon makes a chai so perfect Jonathan and I will fully

93

devote ourselves to it, not even picking up our books again until we have drained our glasses.

In the evenings, the two of us sit by the fieldstone fireplace in the parlor trying to decide which apple trees to order for spring planting. Bits of ribbon and wrapping paper float near our feet. We did some tidying on Christmas morning, but these days are too precious to waste on heavy cleaning. It isn't every day we can spend hours by a warm fire reading a litany of apples while ribbons twist around our ankles. I study the flavor profiles and make a note of early-, mid-, and late-season harvests, but truly I am seduced by the names. *Accordian*, *Annette*, and *Arkansas Black*. *Lady*, *Liddy*, and *Longstem*.

I am dreaming of the day I will make an apple pie with our own apples. Jonathan and I have always celebrated Christmas with pie, though this is only because Jonathan prefers pie over birthday cake. We also sing "Happy Birthday." Not to Jesus, appropriate as that may be. To Jonathan. Because my husband was born on Christmas Day. Then, three days after celebrating Christmas and his birthday, we celebrate again. This time we celebrate our wedding anniversary.

Fifteen years before moving to Maplehurst, we were married on an unseasonably warm, humid day in central Texas. Fifteen years ago, we had a romance. By the time we celebrate our anniversary at Maplehurst, we have a shared life. We have memories; we have children; we have plans. We are sleep-deprived and haven't had a night out in ages, but we continue to dream dreams about the future at a table sticky with maple-syrup fingerprints. This is love in the flesh. This is God with us.

The work of belonging to one another is exactly that: work. We have learned that lesson over fifteen years together. But we are only just discovering that the opportunity to belong to a particular place is also work. This isn't to say that it is laborious. Like marriage, it might sometimes be as easy as Christmastide evenings spent together reading plant catalogs and drawing up lists of heirloom fruit. But the work of belonging does require intention and effort.

Time and space are not such separate entities as we tend to imagine. Days and places intersect, like walls joining together to make the house in which we dwell. We recognize the truth of this when we pray for a white Christmas. We understand how much it matters when we choose to mark another birthday around our old, familiar table. This year, as we celebrate special days, we are learning how to cultivate time in our new home. We are learning how to tend a year by planting ourselves within its days.

I know the first thing we will plant come spring will be tiny, dormant apple whips. But we have already begun planting the year. Each celebration is an Ebenezer stone, marking encounters with eternity we can return to year after year. They are like apple trees. They will change and grow, but they will, God willing, bear their fruit every year, in season.

Our Ebenezer stones placed at Maplehurst this month include a nativity walk. A birthday coconut cream pie. And an anniversary dinner ordered from a local restaurant. We put the kids to bed and eat at the coffee table in front of the parlor fireplace. Tonight I have no wish for a babysitter. I want only our own table, only familiar flames casting familiar shadows. The food is a little cold, and our legs, curled beneath us, begin to go numb.

Gardens are born in winter. Not only in fireside dreams, but also in the messy work of tending small pots on sunny windowsills. And in the harsh work of planting early seeds in cold soil. On those still-wintry days the wind makes us regret we have traded our fleece mittens for gardening gloves. But if we wait for promising weather to sow our seeds, we will never taste the sweet crunch of sugar snap peas in June.

Does God still walk with us here? That was the question on my heart when winter began. Of course, Christmas is the answer. God with us. Love in the flesh. But I need this truth to be more than some belief to which I ascribe. I want to see with my eyes. I want to taste with my mouth. I want to feel the weight of glory as solid and real as an apple in my hand.

In desiring to see more of God, I struggle against the smallness of new beginnings. I dream of apples from my own trees and forget that such things begin within the tissue-thin pages of a nursery catalog. I forget that everything good requires cultivation. This is, in fact, part of the gift. Cultivation is participation. It is a glimpse of that unity we knew in the beginning. It is the way in which we, too, can walk with God in the garden.

I long to see the glory of God in this place, to taste it even, but for everything there is a season. These are still planting days. These are the early days of small beginnings. Days to sow, quite often in tears, hoping, believing, that we may one day reap in joy.

Once we heard God say, "For the LORD your God is bringing you into a good land . . . When you have eaten and are satisfied, praise the LORD your God for the good land he has given you" (Deut. 8:7, 10). We do just that. Over glasses of wine and takeout containers, we stretch our legs, we say thanks, and we plant our special day in the ground of this new place.

Beneath the Veil

My goal is that they . . . may know the mystery of
God, namely, Christ.

Colossians 2:2

This house does not have a laundry room, but it does have a laundry
niche. You find it by pushing your way through a swinging door
in the kitchen. This doorway once opened out onto a small porch.
Maplehurst's previous owners enclosed the porch to create space
for a powder room and an alcove just tight enough for a stackable
washer and dryer.

The history of the enclosure is still plainly evident. First, there
is a tall window peering back into the kitchen. The glass is rippled
like the surface of a clear pond that has just embraced a pebble.
Second, there is the brick wall surrounding the window. These are
the same red bricks found outside the house, but, in this corner at
least, outside has become inside.

Early in the morning, I stand still in this space for just a moment
longer than usual. It is cold. This odd little nook is unheated, and
I hold my hand against the warmth humming from the dryer. Two

97

sets of winter wear—coats, mittens, hats, scarves—are warming up for the walk to the bus stop.

It is a moment of quiet emptiness that lasts just long enough for me to see these bricks as if I am looking at them for the first time. I notice a chunk of missing mortar, and I wonder who spread it. I wonder who laid these bricks in neat rows more than 130 years ago.

I never question that there is a maker. Just as I no longer question whether the world itself has a Maker. The pattern is too clearly evident. But it isn't enough to know that some hand, long ago, smoothed mortar and settled bricks, is it? I want a name. I want a face. I want a story. I want ears able to hear hidden things. I want eyes capable of seeing invisible things, even the invisible hand of God.

Jesus told us that "anyone who will not receive the kingdom of God like a little child will never enter it" (Luke 18:17). I often puzzle over these words. If I believe what my own children say, then they are about as far from receiving the kingdom of God as are our two barn cats, Piper and Tom Kitten. I try to talk to my children about God and faith, but they look at me like I'm the fool. "I can't hear him," big brother says. "I've never seen him," little brother chimes in.

When Thaddeus comes tumbling through the back door after school he brings a gust of cold, wet air with him. "Where did you meet God today?" I ask, as I struggle to hold all the papers, snack wrappers, and water bottles he tosses my way. "I didn't," he says, with just the shadow of a smirk. But I hold his eye, and I ignore the smirk. "Do you think God let you go to school alone? Do you think he wasn't there?" The smirk disappears. Now he, too, is serious. "No," he says. "But I still didn't see him."

I tell myself that it is a beginning. It is belief, though it is as small as the proverbial mustard seed. But even belief this small can open our eyes. Contrary to what we often think, belief is not the destination. It isn't the journey's end. It is a good pair of glasses. It is a telescope. It is a microscope. When we begin from a place of belief, no matter how small or insubstantial, we can see what was always there, hidden in plain sight.

There comes a moment at the very end of the day. Jonathan calls the children in for hot chocolate. I stay where I am outside, enjoying the sudden quiet left by the children's absence. Enjoying the scrape of the snow shovel one direction and the scrape of the snow shovel back. I am so focused on the path revealing itself, I realize only very slowly that the world has changed. While I have been working, the sun has dropped until it rests on the roof of the house just down the hill.

That is the moment the world reveals its true self. Lifting my head, I can see the air and sky tinted rose-gold. Every snow-covered object now has its gilded edge: the white spindles of the porch rail, the brick path between the driveway and the front door, the cypresses all in a line. Every one of them is pink and gold at once.

That is when the snow also seems transformed. Where it had been smooth white frosting or dollops of marshmallow cream, it now appears to be lit from within. I can see that it isn't frosting or marshmallow or even a soft blanket. It is crystal. Precise and sharp and more beautiful than I had known.

Now, here at the very end of the twelve days of Christmas, the heaviness of waiting for Advent finally lifts. I suddenly know, without any effort, that all the old stories are true. Of course they are. The Maker of this golden glory has come. He has walked this ground, and the world has never been the same. This isn't an old, dying world. This is a world in the process of being made new. This is the truth that has always been hiding in plain sight.

The moment evaporates. The sun drifts just below the line of my neighbor's roof. The world again covers itself in a cold, gray veil. But I have seen something important. I am a witness.

I still do not fully know what it means that we must be like children in order to enter the kingdom of God. I suppose there is a wide river of wisdom in those words. For now, I am content to follow a few tributaries. I remember my own childhood and how, as I played, one small space could crack open to reveal an entire world. The hollow at the base of our oak tree was infinite. It was ample enough for all kinds of dreams and adventures and as many acorns as I could collect. The view I saw from my perch on the lowest branch was endless. Not a view of one suburban backyard at all. When you are a child, you can see everything there is without crossing a fence. You know, even if you do not understand your own knowledge, that invisible wonders are hiding in plain sight.

Here at Maplehurst, I am recapturing something of that childish wisdom. As an adult I have looked out over Rocky Mountain vistas. I have stood on the western edge of Europe on a tiny bit of rock once inhabited by monks. I have gazed across the vastness of the ocean. But the creator God I sensed in those places is here too. He is here fully, in all his infinite splendor. The seasons change, the light shifts, the old glass in the window ripples in some new way, and I see what I have never seen before. New shades of the invisible.

And what is the name of this hidden mystery? He has many names. Prince of Peace. King of kings. But I love the name Emmanuel, God is with us. It is a name, and it is a story.

This Place Marked by a Star

When they saw the star, they were overjoyed.

Matthew 2:10

On Epiphany, I dismantle Christmas. I pull it down in a flurry of pine needles and cobwebby candles. I haul up bins from the basement and sneeze the dust of finished days. This year, at Maplehurst, the season does not fade away. It ends. This end begins with noise and mess and chaos. I give myself one day, one single day, to chase down every curly ribbon blown into some corner. To pack away every ornament handmade with macaroni and glitter.

It would be unbearable to step out from within the sheltered days of Christmas if it weren't for the moment that waits for me. The moment that comes after everything is wrapped in tissue paper and carried back downstairs to the basement. I stand with the vacuum cleaner at my side and watch Jonathan carry out the drying tree that has filtered the window light for so many days.

Then, light, like a great flood of water, pours down upon my head through the window's four rippling panes. "The people walking in darkness have seen a great light; on those living in the land of deep darkness a light has dawned" (Isa. 9:2).

It is our first Epiphany at Maplehurst when I know the light I have been waiting for has come. Like the Magi before me, I have arrived at the place marked by the star, and I am overwhelmed with joy.

But first there is grief. A sign that I am being healed. Weeks ago, I finally gave up trying to nurse my baby daughter. The months of trying to increase, then trying only to maintain, my small supply of milk had locked my mind in a hormone-fueled darkness. My freedom depended on accepting my body's failure. On accepting God's "no."

Emerging from depression is like trying to restore life to a limb that has gone numb. The pins-and-needles sensation feels unbearable. I woke from apathy and cried out my final prayers of anger and disappointment. I threw the fussy tubes and bags of my supplemental formula feeder against the wall. I shut the bathroom door and screamed. Two weeks later, or perhaps more, Thaddeus did a silly little dance in his too-small Frosty the Snowman pajamas, and I laughed.

I found the sound of my own laugh startling. I could no longer remember why I had been so angry. I could remember my disappointment and trouble, but it was as if some sharp knife-edge had dulled. "Arise, shine, for your light has come, and the glory of the LORD rises upon you" (Isa. 60:1).

The Magi saw the star and followed it. No doubt the way was difficult, but I imagine the joy of their arrival was richer and deeper for all they had suffered. Still, there is something mystifying about that joy. I could understand it if the star had brought them to a palace or led them to a scene that made sense. But it didn't. It brought them to a family living at home but not quite at home in their ancestral town. It brought them to an unknown child whose birth had been clouded with innuendo and accusation.

Is it possible for us to walk in the footsteps of the Magi? Is it possible today to follow a star all the way to joy? If it is, the journey must cut its path through darkness. This seems to me the only way. The only way to rid us of all our little, ineffectual lights. Our plans. Our strength. Our self-sufficiency. Until we know, deep in our bones, that only one light will do. Only one light will satisfy. The light that is the glory of the Lord.

And what do we see by that light? As my hormones settle, and my mind begins to heal, I am waking up to a beautiful, ordinary world. The same world that the Christ child, the little boy feted with kingly gifts, also grew to know. A world of tears and laughter. A world of hunger and food. A world of aches and pains and happiness. A world of work and of rest.

Like the Magi, I do not end my journey at a palace. Rather, I wake to lovely old windows sealed shut with layers of flaking paint. I wake to maple trees so tall and aged that they drop bits of themselves, whole branches and limbs, in every winter wind. I wake to snow so clean and bright it brings sharp, sun-burned tears pouring down my cheeks. I wake to sit by an old stone fireplace with a little boy on my lap and the sure knowledge that my to-do list does not really matter. Only this matters. This moment. This place. This is enough.

"Lift up your eyes and look about you: All assemble and come to you; your sons come from afar, and your daughters are carried on the hip. Then you will look and be radiant, your heart will throb and swell with joy" (Isa. 60:4–5).

This, then, is another homecoming. This is the culmination of all the Advent waiting and all the Christmas celebrating. This manifest life. For on Epiphany we know again that the kingdom of heaven has recaptured our world. That an ordinary baby, born to ordinary parents, is the embodiment of God's extraordinary kingship over the earth. And we know again that we have been welcomed into this kingdom. We know that we belong.

Epiphany is the meeting place of miracle and prophecy with ordinary flesh and blood. The flesh and blood look no different. "He had no beauty or majesty to attract us to him, nothing in his appearance that we should desire him" (Isa. 53:2). But in celebrating Epiphany, we celebrate the moment when a hidden truth was revealed. Nothing in my world has really changed, but everything has changed. Once again, I have the light to see by. Once again I have words to pray.

My friend Kimberlee once reminded me that Epiphany has traditionally been a day for saying a blessing over one's home. This night, with the last of the fir needles vacuumed away, my family sits down together in the dining room. We read the story of the Magi, and Jonathan and I give each of the kids a small gift. Just a few simple gifts I held back on Christmas Day, including a winter hat with black and yellow stripes. It makes Thaddeus look like a well-bundled bumble bee, much to his delight. And by the light of one candle, we read the words of the prayer Kimberlee gave me.

"Lord God of Heaven and Earth, You revealed Your only-begotten Son to every nation by the light of a star. Bless this house and all who inhabit it. Allow us to find it a shelter of peace and health. Make our house a place of warmth and caring for all who visit us. Fill us with the light of Christ, that we might clearly see You in our work and play. We ask this through Christ our Lord. Amen."[1]

I ask for no other light to live by than the light of the Magi's star. It isn't a light to carry us away from our everyday lives. It is a light by which we see them truly. By the light of this star, I can see even this place with new eyes. For this is no ordinary house. This is no pile of bricks and mortar. This is an outpost of the kingdom of heaven, and a star has risen overhead.

A House of Brick
and Symbol

He who sits on the throne will shelter them with
his presence.

Revelation 7:15

The basement is dark and cold. The dirt floor is worryingly damp.
But after dinner, I stand there in the glow of fluorescent shop lights
and run my hands across a miniature forest of feathery trees. They
are wisps of green planted in recycled yogurt cups. I have labeled
each cup with permanent black marker. Some say *Lancelot Leek*.
Some *Blue Solaise Leek*.

In April, I will plant them. In late summer and early fall, God
willing, I will tug them from the soil and roast them for soup. They
are food, but of course they are also symbols. They are the color
of fresh life. Delicate as new hope. They seem already to wave in
an unfelt breeze, as if they know they are destined for sunshine
and wind. As if they are alive in two worlds at once.

Lillian wanders downstairs and asks to help. I let her pour a little more water into the trays. I show her how to stick her finger into the dark soil. Does it feel too dry? Too damp? With dirt under our nails, we climb back upstairs to read bedtime stories in the parlor.

We've been reading *The Hobbit* here in front of the fire. All winter we have imagined the terrible flames of the dragon. All winter we have looked into the blackened recess of our own stone fireplace and seen the cozy hearth Bilbo was willing to leave behind.

Candlemas is the hinge between Epiphany and the year's first season of Ordinary Time. It marks the halfway point of winter and calls us to remember that, forty days after Christmas, the Light of the world has come. We do not really celebrate this feast day as a family, but I try always to set aside a new beeswax candle. On Candlemas, I light the candle for the first time as we sit down to dinner. I breathe deeply that warmed-honey smell and say, "Jesus Christ is the light of the world." I help my children to respond, "The light no darkness can overcome."

I am not sure whether or not it was prompted by tonight's prayer, but as we sat at the table together, Lillian began to pour out a story of worry and grief. There is a boy at school, and he has no bed of his own. Or is it that he has no water? No way to wash? She wasn't sure. Couldn't remember. But in the gaps and ragged edges of her story, I sensed deep currents of unknown pain.

Some days that is all it takes. One small story is half-heard and a river of guilt is unleashed. Who am I to sit so comfortably within a fine brick house? Have I forgotten that my Lord, God with us, had no place to lay his head?

The tall candle with its strong, reaching flame is a reminder I always need this time of year. In February, I begin to disbelieve the miracle of spring. I wake to another few inches of snow, and it feels as if winter has staked a claim it will never relinquish.

Cold air puddles on every windowsill. Behind our conversations, the radio murmurs a story about the deprivations of winter in a refugee camp.

The symbolism of home and hearth, of candlelight and lamplight holds a privileged position in Christian spirituality. Yet this seems strange when we remember our homeless, wandering Jesus. We often forget that Joseph and Mary, threatened by violence, fled with their young son to live as refugees in Egypt. But perhaps the value of some things emerges most clearly only when they are taken from us, or we let them go, or we choose to live without.

In the book of Mark, Jesus talked about homes. He described a rhythm of leaving and receiving. Of doing without and of tending well. After Jesus told the rich young man that he must sell all his possessions in order to inherit eternal life, Peter spoke up. You can almost hear the self-satisfaction in his voice: "We have left everything to follow you!" (Mark 10:28). But Jesus did not congratulate him. Instead, Jesus said, "Truly I tell you . . . no one who has left home or brothers or sisters or mother or father or children or fields for me and the gospel will fail to receive a hundred times as much in this present age: homes, brothers, sisters, mothers, children and fields—along with persecutions—and in the age to come eternal life" (Mark 10:29–30).

It seems that we, like Jesus before us, will know trouble and displacement. We will be called away from so many great loves: love of family, love of our familiar fields. But we will also be tasked with the work of cultivating new homes and new fields and new relationships. We will wander. We will come home. But always we will follow.

It is not right that anyone should live without shelter. But exile and poverty are not the only wrongs in our world. Too many of us grow fat on abundant, familiar foods yet starve for want of symbols. We live in solid houses, but do not understand what they mean. We forget the one who shelters us. The one who is the roof over our heads and the walls around us. Bilbo didn't leave his home because it wasn't important. He left because of how very important it was.

I reach for our worn copy of *The Hobbit*, an illustrated relic from Jonathan's own childhood, but somehow Lillian and I become distracted by a library book about chickens. This month baby chicks will arrive at our local feed and lumber store, and we want to be ready. Jonathan hasn't yet built a chicken coop. I don't know the first thing about raising newly hatched chicks in a brooder, but as we read the descriptions of different breeds, like the Barred Rocks and the Buff Orpingtons, I begin to feel something stirring. It's as if I have new energy in my limbs. After months spent sitting still with seed catalogs and Tolkien's tales, I am ready to move. I am ready to work. I am ready to see winter dreams come flickering to life.

In the wilderness we lost some things and surrendered others. Now we have received. We have come home. Yet I am wary of making this house, these five acres, an idol on a pedestal. Symbols die when we lift them up in this way. They sway in heaven's wind only as long as their roots are planted in real dirt.

A garden. A few happy hens. They are such little things. Yet it is in these small ways that we allow a kingdom of plenty and of peace to stake its rightful claim in one more bit of earth. The notion of *kingdom* suggests both a ruler and a realm.[1] Over Christmas, we welcomed the ruler. Now, it is Candlemas. Now, by the light of a strengthening sun, we will begin to work our own small corner of his realm.

SPRING

A Growing Hunger

He turned the desert into pools of water and the
parched ground into flowing springs; there he brought
the hungry to live.

Psalm 107:35–36

The first day of spring approaches our horizon, yet it feels strangely as if the gap between my winter dreams and their springtime fulfillment is only growing wider. The plans that seemed manageable in December as we studied the blank slate of our snow-covered hilltop now seem impossible. I watch as my dreams fracture into doubts.

Jonathan and I drop by the local feed and lumber store and study premanufactured picket fence panels. They are all either flimsy or plastic. Most are flimsy *and* plastic. Meanwhile, a long cardboard box is dropped, without ceremony, near our back door. Cutting open the box, I find four sticks attached to cellophane-wrapped root balls. Our apple whips.

I tell the children we will one day bake apple pie, but they look at those sticks and shake their heads. I'm not sure I believe it either.

111

Still wearing my heavy winter coat, I make an experimental jab at the soil with my spade. I feel the unyielding hardness of the earth shudder its way through my bones. The baby apple trees will have to wait awhile, sheltered from the wind on the cellar steps.

The calendar says spring is on its way, but there are no signs of new life that I can see. In the glare and melt of afternoon, the snow coughs up a wilted kickball. Later, it gives up a rusty sand pail. I search in vain for the green bunny ears of growing bulbs. I worry that I may have planted them too deeply. I wonder if they rotted in those early December rains.

Beneath the bright March sun, I see mud and yellow grass that has been ironed flat by months of snow. Crusty wedges of ice lurk stubbornly in the shadows. I am suddenly convinced that we killed the grass by leaving it smothered for too long by autumn leaves. It is impossible that this grass will ever again turn green and grow.

Should we spend the money to buy a chicken coop, or should we build one ourselves? Will we be able to construct raised beds in the vegetable garden in time for early spring planting? Riffling through the rainbow-colored seed packets that fill a shoebox, I wonder if the basement is too cold for growing anything other than seedling leeks and lettuce. I worry there will be no point in planting anything at all if we have no fence to keep out the hungry deer, woodchucks, and rabbits.

I am sick of winter, and yet some part of me wants only to rewind the clock. To go back to days that now seem easy. Uncomplicated by great desire. Like those days by the fire when I read catalogs of fruit trees and was satisfied with only the poetry of their promises. Desire is cruel, stirring up hunger for unseen things. Perhaps even for unattainable things.

The time of our new church's Ash Wednesday service is penciled on the calendar, but when the day arrives, another snowstorm arrives along with it. We stay home and pray our own prayers, and I try to believe, without the evidence of a gathered community and a familiar liturgy, that some new season has finally come.

The season of Lent has traditionally been a time for fasting. A season in which we cultivate some emptiness within ourselves in order to give God new space to fill. This year, I don't need a fast to create emptiness. I need only the view from my parlor window. I can see mud where the coop is meant to sit. I can see a black mulch-covered space where we hope for raised beds and a picket fence. I can see the smooth, still-naked branches of a giant deciduous magnolia tree.

Only evergreen magnolias grow in the deep South. I was twenty before I ever set eyes on a northern magnolia in springtime bloom. I think it was the most astonishing thing I had ever seen. Mountains and oceans and green valleys may possess grandeur, but nothing else suggests, for me, the intimate beauty of the garden in Eden and its Tree of Life like the spreading limbs of a magnolia tree in early spring. Each branch dances beneath its featherweight of pale pink flowers as if a gauzy cloud of birds or butterflies had descended from the sky. Every tree is a gift, but a magnolia in bloom is a miracle.

I have never seen a magnolia as tall or wide as the tree that anchors the northeast corner of our property. From Elsa's window, I can pick out the tightly closed buds that cover its lacy network of branches, and the sight seems to stoke an impossible yearning. I am so starved for spring, I have almost stopped believing in it altogether. Instead, I hunger for more attainable things.

Whether or not we fast, all of us are hungry. While my children dream of sugar, I wake every morning craving hot coffee and buttery toast. Every afternoon my mind turns toward dark chocolate and a mug of steaming, milky tea. We hunger for food and drink, not once or twice, but every day with regularity. We also hunger for touch and love and happiness. We hunger for purpose and meaning and beauty. Our hunger is new every day.

Yet we are terrified of our appetites. Afraid of our hunger. Desire is a dirty word. Perhaps we are terrified by thoughts of sin and shame and selfishness. Maybe we are haunted by a fear of scarcity. *My hunger is too big. There can never be enough.* We imagine a Lenten fast might teach us to subdue our hunger. To somehow rise above it.

What if our hunger is not a sign of weakness? What if it is a sign that we are image-bearers? For surely our hunger bears the imprint of an even greater hunger. A beautiful, generative, rightly terrifying hunger. This is the hunger of the Trinity. Their desire conceived spring. And stars. And nations.

Even the delicate butterfly wings of a magnolia in bloom.

First, there is longing. Only later is there a feast. First, hunger. Then, harvest. I am hungry for heirloom tomatoes. For Amish Paste and Yellow Pear. I am hungry for green beans. For Royal Burgundy and Slenderette. My hunger is unbounded. I want asparagus roasted with olive oil. I want fresh green salads dotted with strawberries. I want ground cherries in their papery husks and baked apples served with ice cream.

I can never rise above this hunger. To subdue it would be a shame. Instead, I press into it, believing that this hunger is made to be satisfied. We have no garden to speak of, only a flat spread of mushroom compost capped with dirty, icy snow, but faith is being sure of what we hope for and certain of what we do not see.

I am far from certain, but my small faith helps me gather empty yogurt cups and peat pots. It helps me gather bags of soil and a shoebox so well stuffed it has broken the rubber band and sent the lid tumbling across the floor. I dirty my hands and count seeds and ponder the importance of the labels. Will I, planting everything on some far-off day in May, be able to tell the difference between cucumber leaves and squash?

While I work, darkness drops and the wind rises. The hanging lights over the porch begin to twist like terrified animals on their chains. There is nothing cozy about this wild March wind. It sounds too much like something howling to be fed. My little faith falters. Gardening is always an act of faith; the seeds are so impossibly small. But who can believe in green, growing abundance when the wind blows like this?

This is not my first spring, and here is something I know: the day when daffodils emerge is not the day for hope. The day when seedlings show the bright green of new life is not the day for faith. That day came and went. Hope is for the dark days. The days when all you can see is mud and mess, like so many forgotten toys strewn across the backyard. Those are the days when miracles begin.

I have always imagined miracles to be like loud shouts. Like trumpet blasts. But they are secretive. They are more like deeply buried seeds. Easter Sunday is not the day for miracles. It is the day for praise. Every miracle we ever needed, every miracle we ever wanted begins in those forty days of rain. Or those forty wilderness years. Even those forty days in the desert. Always, God is tugging us toward resurrection, tugging us and this whole weary, winter world toward new life. But the way is dark. The road is long. The path is quiet. It is paved with hunger.

I stumble a bit as I carry the tray filled with pots downstairs. The basement is dark, and I cannot hold the tray and reach for the dangling bulb. But there are small sounds to guide me. From deep within this dreary cave, I hear spring. I hear newborn voices singing a hungry song.

There is the amber glow from our newly purchased heat lamp. It gives enough warm light for me to find my potting table. To set down my burden of seeds and desires. I lean over to check. Yes, they have water. And here is a little more food.

By the light of an indoor sun, I am able to see what looks like fluffy dandelions each walking on a pair of tiny twigs. Thirteen baby chicks. A baker's dozen of hopes and dreams.

Beyond the Edge

He makes my feet like the feet of a deer; he causes me
to stand on the heights.

Psalm 18:33

I remember a warm, golden day soon after we moved to Maplehurst. I remember looking out over the long expanse of green grass
that runs along the tree-lined avenue and thinking how well suited
it was for an Easter egg hunt. Half a second later that thought
melted into this one: *we should invite all our neighbors.*

I mentioned the idea to Jonathan, but we both lost track of it
in the swirl of cardboard boxes and Elsa's birth. We found it again
during our long winter evenings and passed the idea between us.
Studying it. Adding to it. It was a possibility. Out there. Maybe.
Just maybe. We could try.

The image of a neighborhood Easter egg hunt has floated in the
air all winter. Jonathan and I whispered about it over the children's
heads at breakfast or under the covers after turning up the dial
on our electric blanket and diving, quickly, into bed. But now it

is Lent. And I feel myself tugging back—hard—on an idea that doesn't seem like mine at all.

I know myself fairly well. I know that I do not like crowds. I do not feel comfortable with strangers. I struggle, mightily, with small talk. I am also cautious. I begin to imagine detailed scenarios involving neighborhood children breaking their legs in the holes made by our resident woodchuck. To put it simply, I am afraid. I am lonely, yet I want only to be left alone.

But the kingdom of God is pretty much the opposite of alone. Also, in the kingdom of God, there is this voice saying, "Do not be afraid, do not be afraid, do not be afraid."

Here in the northeast, winter and spring meet like a cliff and its edge. For days, weeks, the view is endlessly bleak. No matter how hard you strain your eyes toward the horizon, there are no signs of change. Only more snow. More cold. More wind. But something has happened to the light. It lingers. It glows with warmth, even if its warmth can't yet penetrate our puffy coats.

The changing light suggests that this endless winter plain is not, in fact, endless. One day soon, the edge will rise up to meet us, and we will tumble right on down and into a new day. It will be the day we spy the first purple crocus in the grass. The day we realize the buds on the forsythia are swollen nearly to bursting. Then, we know: winter is over, and every day now for month after month will bring us some new loveliness.

I have only the changed light and the calendar. Spring still feels impossible. Perhaps this is why I begin to browse online stores selling bulk plastic Easter eggs. I am still unsure, still afraid, but with winter so firmly entrenched, why not check out our options? I decide that buying two thousand Easter eggs isn't actually a commitment. We can always use those eggs next year. Yes, maybe next year would be better. The baby will be walking. We'll be more settled. Less tired. Not so overwhelmed.

Having given myself a year's reprieve, I click "purchase." I wonder what a box containing two thousand Easter eggs looks like. For good measure, I worry that the package delivery driver might strain his back. When I notice the box sitting on the welcome mat a week later, it surprises me with its smallness. Such an impossibly big idea, such troublesome grand plans contained in a box that looks as if it might be just big enough to hold a new microwave oven.

Dragging the box inside, I tuck it into the cobwebs on a basement shelf. I debate in my head. Yes? No? Good idea? Terrible? Jonathan and I stop talking about it altogether, a sure sign we are feeling the same uncertainty. We are standing at an edge, and we know it. The only thing to do is to print a stack of invitations, quickly, without giving it any more thought. Without really having made up our minds, we hop in the car. We drop one paper, still warm from our printer, at each neighbor's door.

One hundred and fifteen invitations with a clip art bunny at the top.

I keep thinking about the temple curtain ripped in half on that first Good Friday. I keep remembering the enormous boulder rolled right away from the tomb on Easter Sunday. And then I picture this house, this hilltop, cracked open. Torn right open. And everyone invited to come in. In this picture, it seems that something precious has been emptied out and is being passed around. It is a frightening, exhilarating vision.

I stand in the candy aisle of the grocery store. Desperate for some control over all the unknowns and fearful possibilities, I study ingredient lists. Thaddeus has severe food allergies, and I know there might be other children in the neighborhood like him. I want candy without common allergens. No milk chocolate. No nuts. I want candy that won't be a choking hazard for toddlers. And it all must fit neatly inside a plastic egg that snaps shut.

I am seeking, I think, assurance. I feel desperate for guarantees. There are many visits to many stores before I gather a heaping pile of candy, stickers, and temporary tattoos. It is my towering bulwark against everything I imagine might go wrong.

I am walking every day nearer to the edge. I committed myself, almost with a running leap, when I dropped off the first invitation. But there is always this edge running through our lives and our days. It is only an Easter egg hunt, but it is also the cliff edge between winter and spring. The fault line between death and life. It is the line between loneliness, which is easy, and friendships, which will be hard work. I am realizing how frequently we are invited to dive into the unknown. To make a flying leap toward light and life and love. How frightening it always is. And how necessary. And also how well cared for we always are, even if we are never, at least not exactly, safe.

It seems that so much depends on listening to the quietest whispers. *How perfect this long, green avenue is for an Easter egg hunt.* And so much depends on following, even if we drag all our fears and doubts along for the wild ride. I don't think following Christ is like aiming at a tiny bull's-eye on a diminishing target. We are not in constant danger of missing the one right road God has mapped out for us. And yet. Perhaps the mystery who first breathed life into our dusty bones is always ready and waiting to carry us over some new cliff. To draw us deeper into unknown territory and on toward unimagined things. Unforeseen gifts.

The Saturday before Easter, the day scheduled for our neighborhood hunt, is still a few days away when I notice the narrow green shafts. They look like the reaching tips of daffodil or tulip leaves. But I see these leaves where I am sure I planted no bulbs. They are emerging in great, long rows and seem to spread out across one whole side of the avenue. I wonder what is coming. What has been waiting all winter long to show itself this spring?

It Is Unfinished

All the ends of the earth will remember and turn to
the LORD . . . declaring to a people yet unborn: He
has done it!

Psalm 22:27, 31

They say the night is darkest just before morning. I don't know if
this is true, or if it is merely a truism, but it describes Holy Week
exactly. After almost forty days of Lent, we are nearer than ever
to resurrection, and yet we are nearer still to the most devastating
day. It is the day the earth rejects her Maker.

Some might protest. They might say we are not nearer to that
devastating day, only nearer to its memorial. But I am not so sure.
To remember as the earth remembers is a powerful thing. Winter
remembers death and spring remembers life, and on Good Friday
the church remembers that "he came to that which was his own,
but his own did not receive him" (John 1:11).

To remember is to participate. Paul writes that we drink from
the cup and participate in the blood of Christ; we eat the bread and
participate in the body of Christ (1 Cor. 10:16). That is what we

do in remembrance of Jesus. Yet I do not want to remember those horrible cries, "Take him away! Crucify him!" (John 19:15). I do not want to confront my own part in this great cosmic rejection.

From childhood, our spirits quicken to the rhythm of a good beginning. We also understand intuitively that an ending is more than just a convenient stopping point. A good ending is a conclusion that casts its light back, helping us find the meaning in the whole. In the beginning, all things were made through Christ. In him was all life. And the life of Christ was our light. As our light dimmed on the cross, he said, "It is finished." "In the beginning" and "It is finished." They are a perfectly matched set.

We love beginnings, and we privilege endings, but we live most of our lives in some sort of middle. Life is perpetually *un*finished. That is its nature. I want to know what the last words of Christ offer those of us who are still living in the shadow of the cross. Those of us who are living in unfinished places and in the midst of unfinished days.

I want to know. I need to know.

Lent has always struck me as a season of very private devotion. But Jonathan and I want our children to learn something about the terrible road to Easter, and so we are trying a new thing. Jonathan found some old barn wood in a corner of the basement. He used two pieces, each about twelve inches long, to make a simple, weathered cross. On Ash Wednesday, I placed the cross at the center of our kitchen table next to a small bowl of tiny nails—the kind we use for hanging pictures. I have plenty of them because, even so many months after our move, most of our framed family pictures remain stacked against our bedroom wall. I also found a child-sized hammer in Beau's little toolbox and laid it next to the bowl.

Each night during Lent, or as many nights as we can manage, we have taken turns confessing a sin from the day. After confessing, we choose a nail and hammer it into the soft, gray wood of the cross. The sound it makes is startling. It seems impossible for such a small hammer. Such tiny nails.

The confession time has been a lot harder than I imagined it would be. The boys seem to endlessly repeat some variation on "I'm sorry I didn't share that toy." After night one, Lillian hasn't thought of a single confession, and I see my own persistent need to be right mirrored in her face. I, too, have struggled to come up with sins, night after night. I know they are here. I feel them, like a seething ugliness I've mostly managed to hide, even from myself. Yet I seem to lack the clarity to be able to pick them out. To name them. And time after time, the whole thing ends abruptly with Elsa's sudden demand for a bottle and bed.

Lillian and Thaddeus are, at least, fond of our homemade cross but dismayed by the nails. I promise them that though the scars will remain, we will remove every single nail in time for Easter. My plan, though I don't mention it to them, is to decorate the cross with early daffodils for Easter morning. However, I am not sure if there will *be* any daffodils by Easter morning.

I keep bumping up against the echo of Jesus's words: "It is finished." I feel as if I have been waiting six months for my dream to *begin*. I try to list our accomplishments since moving to Maplehurst. There is the move itself. All those boxes were not insignificant. We had a baby. That too was not insignificant. I became depressed. I am recovering. But other than that, I can't think of much. We painted the dining room? We brought home baby chicks? I started a few seeds and have only forgotten to water them once or twice? Listed out, it seems so paltry. Like nothing when compared to our grand visions of hospitality and cultivated abundance.

Since coming to Maplehurst, I have received everything and accomplished almost nothing. I have been given a home. I have been given a child. I have been healed. I have found rest. And all I am able to give back are tiny nails. The nightly pounding of a hammer. And even these I find difficult to hand over. Difficult to name and release.

If *it is finished*, then why does so much feel *unfinished*? I am unfinished. My home is unfinished. Our dreams are unfinished. My children are certainly unfinished. This is adorable on some days and maddening on others. I wonder if I am asking these words to mean more than they can possibly mean. Maybe I am asking them to be bigger than they are.

———

Before *it is finished*, there were other words. As Jesus hung dying on the cross, he cried out: "My God, my God, why have you forsaken me?" (Matt. 27:46; Mark 15:34). The meaning seems obvious, and I have always before been satisfied with the obvious—this is a cry of despair. A cry of abandonment. But this year I have clung to these words for weeks. I have felt how they reverberate like thunder. I begin to see that they are so much bigger than they first appear to be.

They are the first words of a Davidic psalm. And every Jewish listener would have known that they were not the story in full. They were only the beginning, and they invoked a very particular, very familiar ending. Psalm 22 opens with that desperate cry "my God, my God" but goes on to make this powerful claim: "For [the Lord] has not despised or scorned the suffering of the afflicted one; he has not hidden his face from him but has listened to his cry for help" (Ps. 22:24). Jesus felt abandoned. Jesus was never abandoned.

In Jesus's few words on the cross, we find the fullness of a powerful story; we find suffering and despair, *and* we find confidence and hope. The psalm he echoed may open with dejection, but it ends with a proclamation of victory: "He has done it!" (Ps. 22:31). Jesus's cry "my God, my God" is like one of these plastic

Easter eggs we are rushing to fill. Crack it open and there is good news, tucked up inside, sweeter than any jelly bean or gummy bear.

It is beginning to grow dark as we work our way through the piles of candy, but through the dining room window I can see snow suspended in the air. These are the lacy, wet flakes of March. They look more like flower blossoms than snowflakes, and I cannot say with certainty if they are a harbinger of winter or of spring.

I do not know if spring weather or spring flowers will arrive in time for our neighborhood Easter gathering. But I believe the words "it is finished" are so big that they hold every one of our days, even those we have not yet lived. It *is* finished, even when all feels unfinished. Death is defeated. We have been forgiven our terrible rejection, and we can live every moment in the knowledge that there is nothing left for us to do. Only everything for us to receive.

For he has done it.

On Earth As It Is in Heaven

Surely his salvation is near those who fear him, that his glory may dwell in our land.

Psalm 85:9

Jonathan and I have a friend who describes some people this way: "So heavenly-minded he's no earthly good." It's possible he's talking about me. I like to curl up in my armchair by the window, tuck my Bible and journal into my lap, and think golden, spiritual thoughts. I am not so adept at putting those thoughts into practice whenever four children are making their joyful noises all at once.

I pray *thy kingdom come on earth as it is in heaven*, but most days I have no idea what this will look like in my house. Or in my neighborhood. Truthfully, the prayer often seems irrelevant to my house and my neighborhood. I glimpsed the reality and knew that our King had come over the dazzling days of Christmas, but on ordinary days, when I imagine his kingdom, I tend to imagine it as something *up there* or, maybe, *out there*. Far, far out there.

Jesus told us "the kingdom of heaven has come near" (Matt. 3:2; 4:17; 10:7). What could he possibly have meant? Was it only ever relevant to those lucky first-century few? Those within grasping distance of a cloak crackling with divine power? I think not. I don't believe the kingdom of heaven departed this planet when Jesus ascended into the clouds. Yet how easily I forget that following Jesus is less about getting myself and others into heaven and more about making space for heaven right here, right now.

On Monday, I sat on the window seat in Elsa's room and watched the largest snowstorm of the year blow its might against the windowpane. Which makes today, the day before Easter, even more of a miracle. There isn't a wisp of cloud in the sky. There isn't even the hint of a wind. Even the mud left behind by the quickly melting snow has dried up and is ready to cradle, but not swallow, two thousand pastel eggs. For the first time in months, it is warm enough to leave our heavy coats in the closet under the stairs. I have never been so astonished by the loveliness of a spring morning. Nor have I ever been so grateful.

Jonathan woke early and hid our eggs by flashlight. I tossed a few around the perimeter of the house for the littlest hunters, but he had his work cut out for him. Bending and hiding, bending and hiding. I am sure his legs will ache for days. Toward midmorning, we set out dozens of doughnuts. We take turns swatting the children's hands away. The boxes of coffee I picked up earlier still feel warm to my touch. And this: I am no longer afraid. I am not even nervous. When I catch Jonathan's eye, we grin. Like the high school sweethearts we once were, we simply grin.

I can feel myself standing in a blessing just as real, just as warm as the sunshine pouring through the still-bare branches. I am standing in this warm place when I notice dozens, and dozens, and still more dozens of neighbors, every last one a stranger to us. They are flowing like a river through the gap in our back fence.

I don't know what the kingdom of God looks like in every neighborhood. It might look like a pearl. It might look like a lamp. It might look like a wedding banquet. But it is possible that it looks like a child's swing set covered in so many kids you can no longer see the swings at all. It might look like toddlers tripping over eggs while their laughing parents hover overhead. It might look like neighbors introducing themselves and discovering they live only a few houses apart.

It might look like a hundred people, all of them new to the neighborhood because the neighborhood is newly built, gathered together on the first warm morning of spring. Ours is a neighborhood without even a park, without any communal space in which to gather, but this day we are together. And every one of us is smiling, and there are no tears, and each one of us, over and over, is saying thank you, thank you, thank you.

So many smiling faces saying thank you. My own among them.

———

I help Beau hunt for eggs near the house with the other toddlers and preschoolers. But I find so much more than candy-filled eggs. Here is the first snowdrop, almost hidden in a patch of grass near the back door. I ring its bell with the tip of my boot. It may have been here for a week or more already, but I have lately forgotten to keep watch. I have let myself be blinded by snow and cold and candy-shopping and worry. And there is more. A smattering of purple crocus has pushed its way through last year's leaves in the empty flowerbed where the fountain once sat.

A neighbor holding the hand of a little girl about Beau's age introduces herself. She asks if I planted the daffodils, and I can only say, "What daffodils?" She points down the avenue, and I remember all the sharp green points I had noticed there, in that spot where I had planted no bulbs.

Even from this distance I can tell that a handful of early yellow daffodils are just beginning to show their color. I should have realized it sooner. I should have believed the promise of those green shoots in neat rows. But I had not felt able to hope for flowers I knew I had not planted myself. Now it is clear what is coming. An entire hillside, stretched out along the drive, will soon ring with golden trumpets.

Our neighbors stream back home, leaving gifts of Easter lilies and potted tulips in their wake. Between these gifts, the purple crocus, and the early daffodils, there are more than enough flowers with which to decorate our cross. I look forward to surprising the kids in the morning. With flowers, baskets, and chocolate bunnies (even a special dairy-free bunny for Thaddeus). And with a new illustrated children's Bible.

It isn't the same illustrated Bible I remember so well from my own childhood, though I spent quite a bit of time searching for an old, used copy online. But perhaps that is best. The picture I remember most clearly from that book now seems misleading. Or perhaps there is some fault in my memory. What I remember is an image of Jesus ascending to heaven on pink-tinted clouds and the words "I go to prepare a place for you."

No wonder I used to imagine Jesus like some sort of celestial carpenter, hammering away at mansions on golden streets. Now I know that Jesus did not speak those words at his ascension. He spoke them just before his crucifixion. It was on the cross that he prepared a place for us. It is the cross that makes our homecoming possible. It is because of the cross that we need not wait any longer to embrace the promise Jesus made to his disciples the day of his arrest: "Anyone who loves me will obey my teaching. My

Father will love them, and we will come to them and make our home with them" (John 14:23).

This spring day rings with joy, like the sound of one snowdrop bell. It tastes like joy, like doughnuts and jelly beans and hot coffee shared with neighbors. It shines with joy, like the soft shades of a thousand eggs. Filled to the brim with joy, I know that the kingdom of heaven is in our midst. I know that the earth, once lost to sin and death and darkness, is returned to us. And to God, its rightful King.

Not fully, perhaps. Night still casts its shadow. Yet that shadow is shrinking steadily. One day it will disappear altogether, and this Easter joy will be everything. Then we will know what we have only glimpsed, what we have only tasted here and there. We will know we have come home.

There Is a River

There is a river whose streams make glad the city of
God, the holy place where the Most High dwells.

Psalm 46:4

I can see spring pouring itself out in my mind's eye: from snowdrop
and crocus through daffodil and tulip and all the way on to snap
peas and strawberries ripening in June. Could any other ending
taste as sweet? The whole season is laced with sweetness. It is the
sweetness of sunshine on an April day when the temperature suddenly soars to eighty. It is the sweetness of green grass—soft, new,
green grass, where I thought green grass might never grow again.
It is the sweetness of my baby daughter's bare white arms. It is the
delicate curl escaping from the lacy bonnet I crocheted for her in
the wilderness, long before I knew her name.

Elsa Spring sits beneath the towering magnolia tree in a pile
of leftover plastic eggs. Beau tosses them in the air over her head
and she laughs. Her laughter sounds like water. I sit only a few
yards away with my camera in my lap, and I can see hundreds of
purple and white violets splashed across the lawn. I follow the

133

flowers with my lens and find violets bubbling up beyond Elsa's blanket and the circle of eggs. They are the beginning of a river of flowers that pours down the line of maple trees and on toward the distant road.

I laugh, too, and I gather Elsa and tug Beau's little hand, and we run toward the sweep of daffodils that has filled one whole bank along the driveway. The narrow land on either side of the long drive moves north to south in a level expanse from the country road to the house. But from east to west, from one side of the looping fence all the way around to the other, it slopes. First gradually and then quite sharply where the driveway cuts its path.

Beau and Elsa and I walk slowly along the split-rail fence, the highest portion of this finger of land. As we walk, we look down on the daffodils that fill the steepest portion of the incline nearer the driveway. It is as if we are walking above the stars. I pull Beau to a stop and turn his shoulders, facing us both back toward the house. Then we take in the sight. The sight I have waited for all winter.

But perhaps I have been waiting my whole life to see this century-old magnolia tree in bloom. From this distance, from this spot above the daffodil stars, we see a dancing tree. Saucer-shaped flowers dip and nod. It looks as if hundreds of pink birds have landed on the branches and are fluttering their wings in the breeze.

We see God's glory. The glory that fills heaven and earth.

Ever since the day of the Easter egg hunt, I have been tempted to use one particular word. I am tempted by the sunshine and the cool breeze. I am tempted by the miracle of this flowering tree. I am tempted by the sight of the new chicken coop that now sits just at the edge of these limbs and their pink saucer blooms. We were able to buy it secondhand from an Amish craftsman who gave it a fresh coat of green paint. I am tempted by the first slight pea vines winding their way up and out of the very first raised bed in our vegetable garden. There is no fence, and Jonathan has eleven beds yet to build, but still I am tempted.

I want to say, but then I do not say: it is *perfect*. I talk myself down from that word every time. Because tomorrow it will be cloudy, or later this week it might freeze. If it does freeze, these perfect pink saucers will droop and brown. The glory of this tree will vanish. But I confuse perfection with permanence. Whoever told me that perfect is only perfect if it lasts?

Elsa is a good and perfect gift. When, at three months old, she started sleeping all night and taking three long naps a day, I asked her to stay that age forever. When, at six months old, she began sitting in our midst with smiles for every person in her family, I begged *please, just stay, forever*. Now, she is seven months old and beginning to crawl, and this, too, seems just about perfect. Because perfect isn't permanent.

I hold Elsa in my arms above the swirl of daffodil stars, and the perfection of the moment is almost too much to bear. I used to think that earth was the place of imperfection and heaven the place of perfection. I used to think that this life was imperfect and death was the door toward perfect. I used to think that this world was change and impermanence, and that other world? That's where everything stays the same, *forever*. But I no longer think it is quite so neat. I no longer believe the dividing lines are so thickly drawn.

Elsa is my fourth child. This means I am under no illusions. I know that even if I write down every memory in her baby book, I will forget. A day will come, sooner than I imagine, when I will find myself unable to recall the particular shade of pink in her cheeks at seven months old. Was it an exact match for the saucer blooms or not? And I will no longer be able to recall how my baby's laughter bubbled like a stream.

Spring is built entirely of such small but essential things. Tiny violets. One sparrow in a cloud of yellow forsythia. An overlooked Easter egg with stickers still inside. But in five years, how much will I remember of our first April at Maplehurst? Will I remember the sweet taste of gladness after months of bitter tears? It sometimes seems that the most important things in life are only rarely weighty enough to settle permanently in our memories.

For instance, just when I have entirely forgotten them, the morning glories return. I spy a pair of heart-shaped leaves emerging in the soil near the red bricks of the front steps, and I am sure I have seen them before. Green leaves and deep purple flowers will twine themselves around the spindles of the front porch. Though the morning glories died last fall, died utterly to the tips of their roots, they managed to scatter their seeds. Now they are reborn. Now they are sprouting and stretching and reaching for the same spindles of the same front porch. They are the most ephemeral of flowers. Yet, somehow, they are the most enduring. They are, in their own way, eternal.

For so much of my life I have sought eternity by keeping my arms wrapped tightly around solid things. Permanent things. Things known and understood. Things sure to last. These are the things I believed had *eternal significance*. But this first spring at Maplehurst is showing me just how much is left out when we equate eternal significance with permanence.

I am discovering that I touch the far horizon of forever when I step forward into emptiness, seeking, like the twirling vine, things unseen. Unknown. Imperfectly understood. We seek eternity like those vines reaching for the home, the source they have never actually touched. And it may be that the most ephemeral of beauties—a baby's pink cheeks, a tree's pink flowers—are the very things to lead us home.

It may be that eternity is the home of so many things I have forgotten or misplaced or failed even to notice. Certainly, eternity is God's home. The throne room of the one who counts hairs. Bottles tears. Holds sparrows as they fall.

Spring is a season unlike the other three. Like the morning glories, it is more ephemeral, yet also more enduring. It is a river that runs through the whole year. We glimpse it when snowflakes fall, fresh and new, like apple blossoms. We see its echo in the brilliant colors of autumn leaves. We feel it on our skin every time a breeze cools the summer air. Spring is the river that bubbles up in the wilderness. It is the river that flows in so many corners of my ever-shifting, always changing life.

Spring is a perpetual season. Its eternal roots lie within the very first Easter, like the few golden daffodils I tucked into our scarred, wooden cross. Jesus was a seed, planted in death and sprouted in resurrection, and that seed has been growing ever since. Because of Jesus, the Christ, who was and is and is to come, we are living a spring with no end.

The river of spring is pouring itself through this day, and I am newly determined. When perfect bubbles up, I will not avert my eyes. I will not bury that freshwater in a flurry of doubt and pessimism (*it won't last, it isn't real, nothing is ever perfect*). Instead, I will dive in. Because this is the river that carries us home.

The Word of the Lord

No longer will there be any curse.

Revelation 22:3

Winter and summer are destinations. You hurtle toward them through the mad-dash days of spring planting or autumn apple picking only to find that you have landed. You have arrived. And, like it or not, you will be staying for quite some time.

But autumn and spring pour themselves out like churning water. You step into the current and attempt to hold it. You try to keep these swiftly pouring days, but they are water. The best-case scenario is that you will splash and swim and drink till your stomach aches. Then, suddenly, before you are at all ready, the water will toss you, indifferently, on a hot, sticky shore. Or a cold one.

No matter the season, we privilege *balance* and *moderation*. But creation scoffs. If we would listen, she would tell us to save our moderation for long summer days or lingering winter nights. Spring, especially, is for the extravagant. This season is for those willing to go all in.

It is late April, and I have abandoned my books. My devotionals, my prayer books, even my Bible are looking at me with neglected covers and untended, dog-eared pages. Checking in on the growth of the pea vines (a task much like watching for the kettle to boil), I worry over the pendulum swing I have made since Lent. From a winter of words, in nursery catalogs and Tolkien's tales, in prayer books and my Bible, to this spring hustle of digging, planting, weeding, pruning. From contemplation with Scripture to contemplation with spade and watering can.

There was a period when I would have narrowed my eyes on hearing someone say they felt closer to God outdoors than in a church. I was sure, and I am still sure, that we mostly find God in the rubbing of shoulders with other, difficult people. People like ourselves. God shows up in the jagged edges between us. I believe this.

But if someone said those words to me today, I like to think I would listen. That I would keep my heart soft and my ears open. Because I have learned how much I miss when I assume God speaks only on Sunday mornings and from a pulpit. Pulpit words. Hymnal words. Devotional words. These aren't the only words in which to hear God's voice.

It seems I have not left words behind though I have temporarily set aside my books, though a little boy with a cold kept me from attending church this past Sunday. I step outside. What do I hear? *Light. Sky. Land.* I pull back the sod and search for hidden things. Long-buried voices. *Seed. Sprout. Bloom.* Some of God's words can never be heard unless we set aside our books, quiet our usual prayers, and look. Listen. Wait.

Then we find them. They may color forth only for a day, but they are eternal. They are his words, spoken from the beginning.

Each day, Jonathan and I run a race against the sun. The sun is growing stronger, the days always longer, but our appetite for work shows no signs of slowing. Somehow, in the midst of Jonathan's day job and caring together for the kids, we are building raised beds in the vegetable garden. Jonathan finishes one, and while he moves on to cutting and setting boards for the next bed, I fill it with compost from a quickly shrinking pile. Right away, I scatter it with seeds. We urge each other on. We work a little longer, always hoping we can work faster than the tomato seedlings in the basement can grow.

I hesitate even to call this work. But what other word is there for the effort that is altering this forty-by-forty plot of ground so dramatically? What other word should I use when we wake every morning stiff and sore? I suppose *pain* is one word I might use. My muscles ache, yet somehow the feeling is a good one. Sore but satisfying. I feel as if I have stumbled on some experience our language does not recognize.

In my memory of Scripture, work is a cursed thing. It is the sweat and toil of Adam's life after Eden. But a quick glance at the book of Genesis shows me the fault in my recollection. In the first chapter of Genesis, God created the world. In the second chapter, God planted a garden in Eden, then he took the man he made and settled him in the garden "to work it and take care of it" (Gen. 2:15).

Elsewhere in the Old Testament, these same verbs are used to describe the work of the priests in the temple as well as God's charge to all his people to keep, or care for, his commandments. Adam's work in the garden is holy work. Far from being a burden, it is a calling. It is his purpose for being in the world. It is a good gift.

Eden was the first temple—a garden temple where God walked with us. Now we live in the after days of Adam's curse. Jesus broke this curse forever when he gave his own body to be broken for us. By his wounds we and all creation are healed. Our bodies are temples, and God is here with us, in this place. No wonder this work feels so right and good. We are planting strawberries.

141

We are sowing seeds for carrots and chard, and in this way we are caring for God's dwelling place.

The work of keeping and caring is various. I am finding it, this spring, in the garden, but surely I was at it all winter. When I made soup to feed my sick child, when I folded laundry to clothe my family, when I swept my kitchen floor, when I made time for relationships through emails or Christmas cards, all of it was the holy work of keeping.

Too often I see this work as drudgery. I sweep the floor and then scream in frustration when my son tracks dirty snow into the house. How many times have I yelled, "What is the point in trying? This work is never finished!" But of course it's never finished. Just as the sun is never finished, it returns every morning, and spring is never finished, it returns every year, and my hunger is never finished. There is always more good food to grow, to prepare, to enjoy. The work of keeping is never finished, and every day there is worship to give.

Some jobs evoke more the "painful toil" of Adam's curse than the joy of Eden's worship. I don't think I will ever like cleaning floors, and I will always be grateful for a husband who tackles dirty dishes with zeal. Sin still has a hold on me, and weeds will no doubt soon rear up in these new raised beds. Yet there are glimmers of Eden everywhere. Like this—the first white flower on a twirling, curling vine.

It is one more word of the Lord. Climbing its way slowly to the top of the lattice we have erected in the raised bed. It is the emblem of the worship I offer, here, in our garden. This flower and the sugar snap pea pod it will become belong to neither the realm of work nor of rest. Instead, they are the fruit of both. When I eat them, I will say, as Ezekiel once said, that the word of my God is "as sweet as honey in my mouth" (Ezek. 3:3).

The Word of the Lord. Thanks be to God!

A Storm and a Bridge

Weeping may stay for the night, but rejoicing comes
in the morning.

Psalm 30:5

Even in spring, the world will keep falling apart. It is sometimes so
terrible I think I cannot go on. Bombs explode or guns are aimed
at children, and an unimagined horror becomes our new reality.
Sometimes it is only a pebble in my boot, a child apparently born
without an indoor voice, or the discovery that it is, in fact, possible to ruin brown rice, even when I use an automatic rice cooker.

Sometimes it is a Friday afternoon thunderstorm that sounds
like a nightmare but disappears after only fifteen minutes. Once it
passes, we step carefully out of the house. It looks as if a careless
child has scattered tree branches and whole limbs like pick-up
sticks. Worst of all is the sight of one immense maple tree lying
stricken across the lawn.

The following morning, we wake to a sky washed blue by the
rain. We had planned to begin work on a picket fence for the
garden, but there is other work to do today. I watch as Jonathan

carries his chainsaw across the yard. His face is gloomy, dark like yesterday's storm clouds. Lillian sees me on the porch and runs toward me, crying. Noticing her tears, I feel only exasperation. I want to swat her sadness away like an irritating fly.

"The tree was already at the end of its life," I explain. "It was only a matter of time. Nothing to cry about."

I have read a lot about maple trees this year. When it was first built, Maplehurst was planted with silver and Norway maples, and these trees have a life span of 100 to 150 years, at most. The house itself is 132 years old, and I have learned to do the math. I know our trees are dying.

I remember the real estate brochure we browsed when we first visited the house last July. I remember how it touted the "maple-lined avenue." I imagine that truth in advertising would dictate a few changes. Not *property for sale* but *caretaker desperately needed for geriatric trees.*

Our trees are dying. I say it, again, to myself, *our trees are dying.* I study the fallen tree. It still waves green leaves, but it is dead. Hollowed out by age, yesterday's wind tore the trunk in a jagged line, as if that great tree had been secured to the ground only by a zipper. Now the trunk is separated forever from the roots that continue to reach toward the sinking drops of yesterday's rain.

Lying in our midst, this tree is more magnificent than ever. I can hardly believe how small my boys seem standing beside the trunk. Joining them, I discover that it is too massive even for me to climb. Only by approaching from the slope above and giving Thaddeus a great heave up, am I able to help him scale the trunk and pose for my camera.

Seeing him there through my lens, I am taken by a sudden urge to lift him off. As if the two of us are shouting in a cathedral or playing silly games in a graveyard. Perhaps this tree is worth the gloom on Jonathan's face. Maybe it is worth even my daughter's great sadness. Could my own optimism, my murmuring about "the circle of life" and "we knew this would happen eventually" be a kind of blindness? A refusal to see and acknowledge that all is not as it should be in this world?

───────

It has been only two months since we planted our four baby apple trees. I look forward to planting so many more trees. I have made a list of them in the journal I keep for the garden: white dogwood and yellow magnolia and evergreen Norway spruce. Red maple, peach, plum, and at least one winter hardy fig. I dream especially of the elusive beauty of the Carolina silverbell. I have seen these trees only in books, but I hope to find a specimen one day. I have already chosen a spot for it on the sheltered, eastern side of our porch.

New life is easy to celebrate. That joy is instinctive. But I wonder if there is something good to be found in keeping and caring for dying trees. If there is one thing Easter teaches, it is that dying matters more than we imagine. Yet also less. Less, because it is not the end we sometimes think it is. More, because so much depends upon death. So much depends upon the death of even a kernel of wheat.

A caretaker for the dying, I think, with my hand on the rough bark. I have seen this fallen tree as a headache and a hassle. And I am sorry.

───────

The tree is lost, and that is a terrible thing. But it is not the only thing. Now that it is night, and we have finally laid our weary bodies down, I have time to remember what else the morning brought. I remember my surprise when two people climbed through a new gap in the split-rail fence. There is an old cherry tree in that spot near the small red barn. One of its limbs fell during the storm and dislodged the top rail of the fence.

They stepped carefully, and I noticed that each was carrying a chainsaw. "We thought you could use some help," she called out. "I wouldn't mind the chance to use this!" he said. He held that heavy saw like a baseball player preparing to hit a home run. They stayed for hours, and we laughed while we worked. They had been out of town Easter weekend and missed the egg hunt, but they were so glad to finally meet us. It is only the fence and the red barn between our two houses.

Lying in bed, I think especially of what Beau said after they had gone. "Look, Mom! Look!" He yelled but with a smile, as if he had made some great discovery. "It's a bridge!" And I saw then what he saw. How the limb of that cherry tree looked, lying across the newly made gap in the fence. It did look like a bridge. He pulled my hand until we stood just beside it. "This is a bridge for two people," he said.

I turned to him in surprise and wondered that such a small boy could see so much.

Disappointment (Such Good News)

The towns will be inhabited and the ruins rebuilt. . . .
This land that was laid waste has become like the
garden of Eden.

Ezekiel 36:10, 35

For my entire life, I have heard Christians say, "This world is not our home." And the Bible would seem to back them up. We are "foreigners and exiles" (1 Pet. 2:11). And "here we do not have an enduring city" (Heb. 13:14). Yet, somehow, I have never heard these words without feeling my heart go cold and numb. I hear them and suddenly feel as if the only way to live is to skate across the surface of life, as if we merely pitch our tents on a frozen river. Why sow seeds, why put down roots, why water the earth with affection if this place can never be our true home?

The longer I live at Maplehurst, the louder, the more insistent, these questions become. Why prune a maple tree carefully in order to extend its life? Why grieve when an ancient tree is felled by a storm? If we are only passing through this place, why bother? Perhaps I should cancel that appointment with the arborist and send the money to a missionary instead. Perhaps I should read my Bible more and my seed catalogs a little less.

Of course, there's nothing to stop me from doing both. I can care for trees *and* orphans. I can garden *and* lead a Bible study. But there is always a choice to be made—with every penny and every minute. If all these things must be weighed in some spiritual balance, then it is difficult to see how the trees might ever come out on top.

In Scripture, it is always the trees that sing. It is the trees that clap their hands for joy. But lately I can't help but wonder what they have to sing about. I do not think they have heard the news. They must not know that the earth, their home, will one day "wear out like a garment" (Isa. 51:6).

The southern slope of our hilltop no longer belongs to Maple-hurst. From the wide windows on the kitchen's south wall, I can see the split-rail fence that circles the back edge of the property. The window centers exactly on the gap in the fence where our neighbors entered for the egg hunt. Beyond the fence and the gap is a grassy spread that flows down toward the sidewalk and the street. On the other side of the street are the faces of the houses that greet me every morning when I stand at the kitchen sink to lift the blinds.

The grass between our fence and the sidewalk is held in common by the new neighborhood homeowners association. It is dotted with a few silver maples, but they are trees without a keeper, and their trunks are girded with thick ropes of poison ivy. The space is also dotted with the tumbled stone ruins of the farm's old out-buildings. From the kitchen, I can see one small, square building without a roof. Vines of Virginia creeper spill and tumble through its two empty windows. I always turn my head, a little startled, when the quartz stones of its walls catch the southern sun.

If I walk down through that gap and move a few steps to the left, I will find myself standing in the great rectangle of the old barn's foundation. This was once a stone bank barn, but the bank, where hay wagons rolled up with their loads to the barn's second-story loft, remains on our side of the fence. Only the fence and a thicket of weedy trees and wild roses keep my boys from tumbling down from the top of the bank and on through empty space.

Tucked back against the hillside are also the remains of a smoke-house and something else that appears once to have been a cellar or cistern. There are another two tumbledown walls a few yards to the west. My kids have taken to calling the entire collection "the ruins." We always take our visitors down for a walk amongst the jagged walls, and we sometimes pose against the pale yellow fieldstone for photographs. I have forbidden my children to play there unsupervised.

I cannot see these stones without thinking of the first farmers at Maplehurst. Were their hopes and dreams realized in this place? Would they be devastated to see how their hardworking structures have crumbled, almost into nothing? I wonder, too, if Jonathan and I are building anything more enduring. I look around and know that not even stone walls can be counted on to last.

On most days, it feels as if we can make no headway against chaos. While a garden of raised wooden beds slowly emerges in the sunny spot by the small red barn, the wood around the third-floor windows continues to rot. And one day this month, my boot finally breaks through the soft spot on the porch. Everything falls apart. Nothing lasts. And life sometimes feels like a daily exercise in managing my expectations. Every sweet thing is laced with the bitter flavor of disappointment.

There are days when my eyes are dazzled. By a moon like a heavy silver pearl, or a rainbow, broken and splashed across the wall. By the magnolia tree in bloom, as magnificent as the Tree of Life. But those days are the exceptions. In this place, I begin each day at the top of the stairs. And every single day, as I descend, my hand catches on the rough scar made by a disobedient little boy who once slid belt-buckle down despite the warnings, despite the rules. Every beautiful thing is edged with brokenness.

The writer of Hebrews reminds us that "here we do not have an enduring city, but we are looking for the city that is to come" (Heb. 13:14). I read these words, and it is suddenly as if they are illuminated. They are no longer dark and cold. It is true that we do not yet possess an enduring home, but *we are looking for it.*

We are watching and waiting and straining to catch a glimpse of the coming of that which John saw: "The Holy City . . . coming down out of heaven from God" (Rev. 21:2). And I am beginning to see. Perhaps because it is spring, or because we are still singing Easter hymns each Sunday, but I am beginning to see small glimpses of my forever home.

I have seen a magnolia tree like a miracle and a storm build a bridge for new friends, and I realize Isaiah's words are a promise for today: "See, I am doing a new thing! Now it springs up; do you not perceive it?" (Isa. 43:19). And I do. I begin to see it.

We were never made for heaven. Our bodies, formed of dust, were always intended for a life on earth. This world *is* our home. The great promise has always been not that we would go to live with God, but that God would come to make his home with us. Yet we taste the bitterness of disappointment because our home is not yet as it will one day be.

We catch sight of it here and there. We hear the word *shalom* whispering in the treetops. We take up our spades, and we make room for it. We cast seeds, and we plant heaven on earth. We watch and wait for all that God will grow.

One day, as we read in 2 Peter 3:10, God will cleanse this world with fire, as he once cleansed it with floodwaters. The earth will be like a mountain meadow after a raging forest fire. All the old, decayed things will be gone, and our resurrected eyes will be dazzled by the new, beautiful green of spring. Our resurrected ears will ring with the music of trees.

In the light of this promised future, death loses its sting. Even my daily disappointments lose their sting. For what is disappointment but the reminder that *this is not all*? That there is so much to look forward to? This banister is scarred, but one day we will make beautiful things out of warm wood, and they will remain beautiful. Nothing will mar their loveliness. In that day the only scars will be those Jesus still bears. In God's kingdom, a temple is destroyed, and only three days later it is rebuilt.

I study the emptiness where the soaring roof of a great barn once blocked out the sky. Except, it isn't empty. A slender tree has grown up through a large crack in the precise center of the barn's foundation. Nearly as tall as the barn once must have been, it has almost no limbs. Only a tall, willowy trunk and a crown of delicate green leaves. It's as if, when the roof tumbled down and the sunlight poured in, this tree leapt for joy.

An Ancient Song, Always New

"You are my witnesses," declares the LORD, "that I am God."

Isaiah 43:12

It starts when we are so young. When we are only just beginning to know the world we have been born into, someone, some well-meaning teacher or visiting aunt perhaps, asks us the question that will haunt us for years: What do you want to be when you grow up?

My own answer was always changing, usually in response to some moment that felt, even as I lived it, like a crossroads. Like the middle school assignment that required me to interview someone in my chosen field. Later, there was my choice of university and my choice of major. Still later, there was my choice of academic specialty.

To each choice I brought my longing for significance. I wanted, as we all want, to do something with my life that mattered. Because I was raised in the church, every decision and every dream was

153

tainted by my deep-rooted suspicion that only a few occupations really mattered. Preacher. Missionary. Evangelist. Alas, all three were roles I felt ill-suited to fill.

I am determined not to burden my own children with that question. I am determined to teach them, with my words and with my life, that their purpose is already known. Their purpose is already secured for them.

Lillian and Thaddeus. Beau and Elsa. I know what you have been made to do. Like Adam, like Eve, you will be priests.

———

Of course, they won't understand. Not at first. I hardly understand it myself, but it is becoming clearer to me here at Maplehurst. I have begun to see for the first time in my life what Peter means when he writes that we "are a chosen people, a royal priesthood, a holy nation, God's special possession, that [we] may declare the praises of him who called [us] out of darkness into his wonderful light" (1 Pet. 2:9).

The garden in Eden was the first temple. God gave Adam, God's first priest, a charge to care for the garden. As priest, Adam received the gifts of the garden. He cultivated and ate them. But in everything he did, Adam offered the garden back to God through the sacrifice of thanksgiving.

When we give thanks, we bless creation; we say, as God once said, "it is good." Even more, our thanksgiving is the recognition that this goodness belongs to God. Animals also take in God's creation as food, but we image-bearers alone take and eat and acknowledge the one who has given it. Our hunger is never fully satisfied by the food itself but only by the God who has given it. The God who feeds us with himself.

We know the ancient story. We know how Adam and Eve failed as priests. They took and ate food that had not been given to them and in this way pursued the world for its own sake and not for the sake of God.[1] But the story that began in a garden also ended in a garden. It ended in the garden of Gethsemane when Jesus willingly gave himself for us: "My Father, if it is not possible for this cup to be taken away unless I drink it, may your will be done" (Matt. 26:42).

But in this "ending" is the seed of a new beginning. In another garden, the garden of an emptied tomb, the resurrected Christ was mistaken for a gardener. And, in a way, he is. He is a perfect Adam. He has conquered that which threatens the good garden of creation: sin and evil and death.

He is our high priest. He is the one who says, "Take and eat; this is my body" (Matt. 26:26). Now we, too, have the right to be called children of God, a royal priesthood. Our first role has been handed back to us, and our garden stretches to the ends of the earth.

A messy, overgrown lilac anchors the northwest corner of our new vegetable garden. I remember noticing shortly after moving in that powdery mildew spotted its grey-green leaves. I wondered at the time if we shouldn't simply dig the whole thing up to clear space for the picket fence, but laziness or hope led us merely to chop it back. It seems the pruning did it good. Today, as I set out my vegetable seedlings and prepare to plant, the lavender scent of lilac washes over me, as if someone has broken a jar of perfume.

The shifting seasons usher in so much redemption, even the redemption of one overgrown lilac. As priests we are witnesses to these redemptions. We are here to receive, to name the work of God's hands, as Adam once named, and to proclaim, "Heaven and earth are full of thy glory!" Today God's glory smells like lilac. It looks like the dance of lavender petals in the breeze. I clip a few scented branches and set them aside in a jar of water. I will give them to our neighbors, a small thank-you for their help after the storm. That, too, is priestly work. To receive, to give thanks, and then to pass it on.

I have never grown my own tomato seedlings before. These tall, heavily scented plants tucked into recycled yogurt containers make me feel like a proud mother. When I brush my fingers over their leaves, my hands take on the smell of summer. Of sauce bubbling in a pot. Of bacon sandwiches piled on plates. Pizzas in the oven. I look forward to the fruit of these plants not only because I want to taste them myself, but also because I want to pile them in baskets and share them with neighbors. There is treasure here.

There is treasure, especially, in these Brandywine tomato seedlings. Brandywines are the most delicious tomatoes, the most like the essential essence of a tomato. When I first tasted one a few years ago, it was like remembering the flavor of something I'd never tasted before. This, I realized, was what I had meant all along whenever I said the word *tomato*.

But this treasure is available only in a garden. You will never find Brandywines in a grocery store produce section. You will not even find them at most farmer's markets. Brandywines have a tendency to crack and split on the vine. This makes them unappealing to market growers but exactly right for Maplehurst, where every day I witness the significance of cracks, scratches, and scars. These tomatoes might break and spill their precious red juice, but how much easier will it be for me to remember the truth of this world and my purpose in it if my hands are stained red?

The best things, the most nourishing gifts, must be broken and spilled and shared. Including our own lives. Christ showed the way. And we follow. We take and eat. We, too, drink from that terrible cup. It looks like death, but it tastes like life.

It is especially strange that we burden children with this question of what they will one day *do*, when so much of our lives is already prescribed. What will my children do? I can already see most of it. They will sleep. They will eat. They will live in relationships with others. They will celebrate special days and live ordinary days that tick with repetitive tasks. The truly important question seems not to be *what* will they do, but *how* will they do it.

Will they bless the food they eat and so receive it within the context of a relationship with God? Will they pursue truth and justice and beauty as things belonging, not to a dark world, but to the light that has come into the world? Will they keep and care for their environments, homes, offices, and neighborhood parks? For their urban centers and national forests and for those who live in them? In these ways and in every moment of their days, will they proclaim the gospel, the good news of Christ's reign and redemption?

Whether they are engineers or writers or gardeners or, even, unemployed or bedridden by illness, I pray they will live as priests in this world. I pray they learn from me and their father what it is to offer with our whole lives the sacrifice of witness. This witness, in word and deed, in happiness and suffering, is always this: God is God, and he is love, and through Christ all can be redeemed. Everything, including our own hearts, can be made new. *Heaven and earth are full of thy glory!*

I am created from dirt. How right and good it is, then, to kneel in this garden temple and sing songs of praise. To see and name as Adam once named. A song of Brandywine tomatoes and French Breakfast radishes. Of mini bell peppers in orange and red and chocolate brown. Of cucumbers for pickling. I sing of Red Flame lettuce, peppery arugula, and dill seeds cast across one bed. This is the oldest song in the world. And it is new every spring.

SUMMER

Let Us Cultivate Glory in Empty Fields

Awake, north wind, and come, south wind! Blow on
my garden, that its fragrance may spread everywhere.

Song of Songs 4:16

I sometimes think that every good gift I've been given has its roots
in emptiness. I cannot separate the blessing of these four children
from the years of infertility and longing. I cannot distinguish this
hilltop from the restless wandering that brought me here. Even
summer is a gift we receive only on the far side of winter.

The home we are making is far from our extended families
and our old, familiar friends. This whole wonderful year has had
a great loneliness running through it. A few months after Elsa's
birth we found a church of our own, but it lies at the other end of
a long drive in the direction of the city. Yet even this inconvenience
is like an empty vessel. When I stop trying to fill my empty places,
I leave room for glory.

161

There is room for a night like this one. A moonlit midsummer's eve and a porch crowded with neighbors. Our long glass table is laid with food from the garden and farm market, and my potting table has been repurposed for sweet, pink drinks. The kids are playing flashlight tag with their new friends. We can hear their happy screams in the dark.

If I lived near family, I would fill my calendar with family. If we lived nearer to our church, I would probably have invited only new church friends. But family and church are far, and we are left with only one option. The best option. We are celebrating midsummer's eve with our neighbors.

Spring swells and ripens and gives us June. The breeze no longer reminds us of winter's icy breath, but the warm afternoon sun is still welcome. The sugar snap peas are fat and sweet on their curly vines. The violets in the lawn have faded, replaced by bright dandelion buttons. The tomato seedlings are settling into their beds and beginning to climb their cages. Baby lettuces lie nestled in perfect rows.

Lillian says the lettuces look like the ones in Mr. McGregor's garden. Here, from one of the black wicker rocking chairs on the porch, I can just glimpse their delicate ruffles in the last of the day's light. I decide that Lillian is right.

I tried and failed to grow snap peas once before. The bitter taste of that failure had lingered, but this past December my hunger for sweet peas reignited when I read the description of Amish Snap Peas in *Seed Savers*, my favorite heirloom seed catalog. Life, I decided, would not be complete until I had tasted this "superb" flavor and "delicate" sweetness.

I planted two neat rows of Amish Snap Peas on a day in late March. Each seed was nothing more than a single, slightly shriveled pea. The next morning I woke and saw my raised bed frosted with a smooth inch of soft snow. I despaired over that snow, sure my precious peas had died of cold. I watched for weeks, convinced they'd never grow.

But they have. They are nothing like the sad, short vines of my first attempt. Back then, in a shared plot in an urban community garden, the white flowers dropped off in the sudden onset of Midwestern summer heat. I had planted them too late. I know now that spring peas must be sown while spring itself remains only an unrealized dream.

A decade ago I lived in a sixth-floor apartment with only a few potted plants on windowsills. What would I have thought if I had been given a glimpse of the life I would live on this hilltop? If I could have seen this house, my family, our neighborhood? If I am honest, I can say that I would have been shocked. And disappointed. I think I would even have been afraid.

I loved my little houseplants, but a vision of those pea vines reaching and curling above my head would not have cheered my heart. Not even the sight of all these flickering tealights, nor all the faces gathered on this wide, wraparound porch. In those days, I dreamed a number of dreams, but not one of them looked anything like this.

In so many ways, Maplehurst is the negation of all the plans I made as a young woman. While I taught classes and struggled to finish my dissertation, I gave little thought to peas, lettuces, and tomatoes. I only rarely made the long walk across campus to water the vegetable plot I shared with a few other graduate students. On difficult days, I consoled myself by imagining an English department faculty office lined with bookshelves. I envisioned a quaint college town. I thought about regular office hours and young people who admired me and called me "professor."

I don't think there was anything wrong with the dreams I was dreaming and the plans I was making. I was where I needed to be, doing work I needed to do, and those dreams kept me there. They kept me hungry enough to persevere. But as my far-off dreams came near, as I searched for a job, graduated, and began teaching part-time, it became more and more clear that my heart and those dreams were not a good fit.

In those days, I stumbled on the words of Psalm 20:4: "May he give you the desire of your heart and make all your plans succeed." I read those words and imagined that my own heart was like a blank sheet of paper. There was not one thing I desired wholeheartedly. I had no plans in which I was confident. At times I did wonder, if my heart was blank, why I still felt such an all-pervasive ache.

I know now that my heart was not blank. It had been emptied, which is a very different thing.

Dreams are a form that emptiness takes. They are the particular, unique shape of our own yearning. The emptiness itself is easy. We are born hungry. Hunger is the language of our infancy. Even adolescence can be summed up as a period of growing restlessness. But it takes years, a lifetime perhaps, to understand what we truly hunger for. To know the precise dimensions of that which will satisfy us.

Too often we try to bypass that hard-earned knowledge with pronouncements. We say only God satisfies. We say every desire is only a misplaced desire for him. But pronouncements, even those laced with truth, are difficult to live. They highlight the end but do little to illuminate the journey. If God is my satisfaction, the end of all hunger, then why, if I think I have discovered him, do I wake on so many mornings still feeling so ravenous?

These were the questions that carried me to Maplehurst. These were the questions that burned in my heart all autumn, winter, and spring. But now it is June. Now my cup overflows. I was hungry, but now I am fed. Fed with sweet snap peas, warm and raw-green from the vine. There is homemade onion dip on the glass table in the corner of the porch. It is laced with smoky-sweet caramelized onions, but these peas need no embellishment. The catalog writer did not exaggerate. They are, indeed, superb.

I am fed, too, with pale pink radishes. We frost them with sweet butter from the dairy a few miles away before we dip them in a dish of coarse salt. I am fed with the warmth of sun-ripened strawberries I bought this morning from the Amish farmer and his little boy in their matching straw hats.

But there is more than good food. There is Elsa on my lap; she is like the presence of spring in every season. There are also the first few buds on the bare-root roses I planted on a whim in early April. Bonica. The Fairy. New Dawn. And that one which makes me strain to remember my college French, Blanc Double de Coubert. It has only one small, half-opened bud of pure white, but the perfume is almost too much to bear.

Earlier today I was on my knees in order to get as close as I could to that heavenly smell when I realized that even a backyard rose can be a burning bush. And surely God is in this place. I have tasted his goodness. I am enveloped by his presence. I know, as I have never quite known, that he is the God who formed me. The God who sees me. The God who knows me better than I know myself.

The ache of winter and of early spring is the ache of exile. The ache Adam and Eve knew so well. Yet it was different once. Adam and Eve knew what they had lost. Their beautiful garden. Their meeting place with God. Their innocence. It is not the same for us. We are born into exile and must learn to recognize what we are missing.

It isn't enough to know that we yearn for God. Somewhere along the way we must also learn that creation is God's good gift. Its true identity is not the chaos and horror we observe on the nightly news. We must learn how to walk with God on the ground of our own lives, how to meet with him in our kitchens and neighborhood sidewalks and backyards. We must become acquainted with the righteousness Christ has made available again. To recognize and release the nails of our sins.

Only then can we begin to receive the life that is to come, the world that is to come. Our hunger is the exile's hunger, but it is also the first step in our homecoming. We hunger and in doing so learn the shape of our emptiness and the world's great emptiness in order to prepare room for God's presence. We imagine we are cultivating food or friendship or beauty. But we are, in all of these ways, cultivating God's glory in our midst. We spread our tables and fill our plates with glory.

I take it all in—the food, the candlelight, the voices—as I rock slowly with Elsa in my arms. And I am full, so full, I am overflowing.

Love, So Slow and Beautiful

Your eyes will see the king in his beauty and view a
land that stretches afar.

Isaiah 33:17

June brings sudden thunderstorms. Every afternoon for a week,
we stand, five of us and the baby on my hip, and gaze at rainbows
in the eastern sky above the small red barn. Once the sun sets
and the children are in bed, Jonathan and I rock, side by side, on
the porch. We keep the lights off and clink the ice in our drinks,
counting stars, picking out planets, and following the trajectories
of swooping, diving bats. Today's storm has blown on, but every
so often lightning illuminates the curves of far-off hills, and we
remember, just for an instant, that the same ground we know and
love reaches on and on and all around the globe.

June days are the longest days we are given, yet they are never quite
long enough. Ready or not, night falls, like a curtain on our starring
role. Nocturnal creatures, like owls, like Venus, take the stage. Thank-
fully, June nights are also the loveliest nights. Soft and warm but not
yet buzzing with mosquitoes. They throb, instead, with starlight.

167

Tonight, the silver moon is nearly full. It shines like a spotlight on the neat, green chicken coop. Despite the long days, the picket fence for the garden remains only half built, but this week constructing an enclosed chicken run along one side of it has become a sudden priority. Our chickens are no longer babies and need a safe space in which to roam. The length of deer fencing we temporarily strung up around the coop is unwieldy. I have an angry red scratch running the length of my arm thanks to that wire. My upper arm is still tender from a tetanus shot.

After several visits to the feed and lumber store, Jonathan and I decided that flimsy, premanufactured fence panels weren't right for Maplehurst. Jonathan is measuring and cutting each thick picket himself. I have watched him this week, working between a stack of wood and the table saw, and wondered if our plan is foolish. This spring and summer, many of our neighbors have installed no-maintenance vinyl decks in their backyards. Meanwhile, we are creating work for ourselves that will only lead to more work. Why not set up a plastic picket fence that will never fade, warp, or ask to be repainted?

For now, the unfenced garden has been largely ignored, but I imagine it is only a matter of time before the woodchucks and rabbits discover this new twenty-four-hour salad bar. I don't even want to think about hungry deer. I wonder if I will come to regret choosing slow, handcrafted beauty over speed and utility.

My plans for a day are always bigger than the day itself. I never have learned to write a to-do list that exactly fits a twenty-four-hour slice of life. Fence-building was meant to be our spring project, but my plans for the season outstripped the season itself. It is beginning to seem quite likely that my plans for this first year at Maplehurst are bigger than the year. I wonder if my dreams for this place are bigger than the span of my own life.

I could fight this reality. I could work harder. Faster. More efficiently. I could cut corners. Prioritize ruthlessly. I could watch the clock and the calendar with vigilance. I could push aside the curtain of the setting sun and keep on going. I could forget about real wood and make friends with vinyl. Instead, I have asked Jonathan to build a clothesline.

There are the pickets to cut and the run to construct, and we do have a gas-powered clothes dryer in the alcove off the kitchen. But when I look at the flat, grassy space next to the asparagus patch, I see a vision of white sheets blowing in the breeze. I see something beautiful asking to be born.

Every beautiful thing has been spoken into being by love. It is made through Christ, for Christ, and is held together by Christ. Sometimes it is given. It is the rainbow in the sky, too large and lovely to miss. But sometimes beauty is hidden; sometimes it is quiet. It waits to be discovered and unveiled. Sometimes it asks us to help create it. Perhaps to build it with wood and a table saw.

I wouldn't complain at all if there were less laundry to do, and yet I am not that interested in doing the job more efficiently. Instead, I want to do it more beautifully. Which is another way of saying, I want to do it with more love.

A vision of postcard perfection brought me to Maplehurst. As if the words *Wish You Were Here!* had been stamped across the image of a bright, white farmhouse, rolling green meadows, grazing animals, and a soaring, red barn. But that sort of beauty is only a dream. In other words, it isn't true beauty at all. It is a signpost, perhaps. Possibly a map. It might be a promise, but it is not the thing itself.

True beauty is not vague or distant. It is not a rose-tinted vision. Beauty belongs to the waking world. If beauty comes from God, then we will not find it in abstraction. It does not live in dreams; it lives in dirt.

Maplehurst looks almost nothing like my postcard vision. It is chipped red bricks and new beige houses crowding a little too close. It is an adolescent chicken strutting across the lawn, oblivious to her awkwardness. It is a red shed falling down, with exactly half of a rusty weather vane tilted against the sky. Some might say that Maplehurst falls short of the ideal beauty I glimpsed in my dreams. But this allegiance to "ideal" beauty is a form of blindness. It is a refusal to lift the veil of everyday life in order to see the glory of God.

What does the glory of God look like? It is, as Ezekiel discovered, as ordinary and utterly extraordinary as a rainbow on a cloudy day (Ezek. 1:28).

Perhaps Jonathan and I will spend our whole lives working on this picket fence. First planning and cutting it. Later painting and repainting it. Far down the road, I'm sure it will need mending. But maybe the cultivation of beauty is a good way to spend one's days. Even one's whole life.

Our aim is not to maintain this house—or ourselves, for that matter—in painted perfection. Our ambition is simply to care for this place and for the people who step through its door. That is what love looks like.

Love doesn't tick boxes on a to-do list in order to live its real life on vacation somewhere else. Love pours itself out, right where it is. Love does things right, does them well, takes care. Of course, I am speaking of fences as well as of children and neighbors. I am speaking of laundry, and I am speaking about all of life.

Who Was, and Is, and Is to Come

I consider that our present sufferings are not worth comparing with the glory that will be revealed in us.

Romans 8:18

In our home, birthdays are for simple pleasures. We do tea parties with the china teacups I inherited from my aunt. We do root beer floats on a blanket in the grass under the sour cherry tree. We bring out the linen napkins I bought years ago in a tiny village lace shop on the west coast of Ireland. We hang twenty feet of bunting I once made from the prettiest scraps in a big bin at the fabric store. We do balloons tied to your chair at breakfast. We do home-baked cakes.

But what happens when a home-baked cake is the only option? If you are a little boy allergic to flour and butter, then you will dream of bakery sheet cakes in garish colors. You will dream of Jedi Knights piped in buttercream. Every year on your birthday you will ask for a birthday cake with a toy on top. You will ask for a cake just like the one they served at your best friend's birthday party at the pizza parlor.

Your mother will do her best. She will try a different recipe every year. She will stock up on almond and rice flour. Coconut flour and even garbanzo bean flour. She will learn how to make marshmallow frosting, and she will color it brilliant blue. She will put a Hot Wheels car on top and watch as it slides, slowly, toward the marshmallow edge. She will do her best, but it will never be the cake of your dreams. It will always taste, at least a little bit, like disappointment.

Thaddeus and I have the same June birthday. But for the first fifteen years of my life, I shared my birthday with my favorite aunt. I think I can say favorite without offending my other aunts because Sissie, as we called her, was unmarried and had no children. This meant she belonged to me and my siblings in a way that my other aunts and uncles never could. She was *ours*. She loved us and was deliberate in helping us to know it.

Sissie died in a car accident at the end of what I had thought was simply one more ordinary June. I had just turned fifteen, and she had just turned forty-five. I had been away at camp when she called to tell me happy birthday. Every one of my birthdays after that was edged with absence. Until my twenty-ninth birthday. Seven years ago, on a June day of cool breezes and cottony clouds, the labor nurse placed Thaddeus in my arms and said, "Here is a son who will never forget his mother's birthday."

Of course, neither I nor the nurse thought then of a young child's innocent self-centeredness. For years I would need to remind Thaddeus that his birthday was also my birthday. Today he turns seven and no longer needs reminding. When I ask him to tell me the very best birthday gift I ever received, he knows the answer is himself.

God does not erase our losses, those empty places in our lives, but he does something almost more miraculous. He fills the loss with a sign of his presence.

———

We are called to make room for the world to come within the womb of the old. This everyday world—this dirt, these trees, our neighborhoods, even our own bodies—are like a mother to the new creation. Is it any wonder, then, that there are birth pains? Always we see the truth of Paul's long-ago words: "We know that the whole creation has been groaning as in the pains of childbirth right up to the present time" (Rom. 8:22).

Because of a brokenness within my own body, my wait to conceive Thaddeus was long and bitter. My pregnancy, when it finally happened, was touched by fear, as if I carried both a son and deep doubts about God's goodness. I felt I owed God something for the gift of this child and so I anticipated a hundred sad scenarios. Only toward the end, as spring turned to summer, did I begin to receive the truth: God delights in giving good gifts and with no strings attached. I should have known my son, this good and perfect gift, would arrive on my birthday. Instead, I was astonished.

Today Thaddeus rides his new birthday bike in circles around the house, lost to daydreams and oblivious to the little brother who screams, "Wait for me! Wait for me!" I look at my older boy and remember our mad dash to the hospital. We lived only a few blocks away, but I was so suddenly overwhelmed by labor pains that I waved Jonathan toward the curb when we were only halfway there. As Jonathan began to slow the car, I was jolted by fear. I could see that if we stopped my baby would be born on the side of the road. I yelled, "Keep driving," and Thaddeus was born less than ten minutes after stumbling through the maternity ward doors.

We sow in tears, and we reap in joy. Always this is true. We cry for a child of our own, and we birth him with a scream, and then we watch as he grows and dreams his own dreams and aggravates his little brother and loves his baby sister with a litany of silly nicknames. Now, every year on my birthday, I relive the exhilaration of childbirth. When my mother calls to talk, I know she is remembering the same. This is the day, more than any other, when I confront the ties of love that bind me to the living and the dead. The old world and the new.

I long to hold Sissie's hand and to hear her laugh again, but I listen to my own child's laughter and know that new life and the glory of the kingdom to come are bubbling up all around us. The new creation, the new earth, and our new, healthy bodies are out there, ahead, and I yearn for them. But their glory is also here, today. In this joy and in this pain.

Last summer, the evening of the day when we first stepped inside Maplehurst, Jonathan and I ate dinner at an Italian restaurant just a few miles down the road. We opened our menus and found gluten-free pasta, bread, and pizza crust. When asked, our waiter pointed out the gluten-free bakery at the other end of the block.

We came back to the bakery the next day. It had an awning over the window the color of chocolate frosting. There were two tiny café tables on the sidewalk. Stepping inside, we discovered that not only did they make their own gluten-free breads, but they also baked cakes without wheat or dairy. We told the owner about Thaddeus, about what this place might mean for him. She told us to wait and stepped into the kitchen in the back.

When she returned, she was carrying a chocolate bakery cake. It was smooth and perfectly round. It was piped with delicate, chocolate roses. "This is the first birthday cake for a baby with allergies," she said. "I can make one for your son too." Our offer for Maplehurst hadn't yet been accepted, but that was the moment when I was first certain this place would be our home.

That was almost a year ago, but I have held on to the promise of that chocolate cake ever since. Today, when Thaddeus saw the paper bakery box, his mouth opened. It stayed a perfect O while I let him peek inside. I suppose I could have made my own wish this afternoon when Thaddeus blew out the flames on seven candles shaped like LEGO bricks, but it didn't occur to me then.

Now it does. A full moon is rising, as bright, I imagine, as thirty-six candles on a silver cake. It has just reached the top pane of the window on the stairs. I look at the moon and touch the rainbow colors on the wall, and I wish what I have wished countless times before. I wish for the coming of the one who will gather up all the lost and broken pieces. And make them new.

Showers of Blessing
(So Sharp and So Cold)

Taste and see that the LORD is good.

Psalm 34:8

I see the world through a lens of metaphor. The old magnolia tree that shelters our chicken coop is a love letter. The rainbow window in our stairwell is a promise. Metaphor enables me to see the world more clearly, like a pair of good eyeglasses. It is the tool I use to scratch beneath the surface of things. I still hope to find a replacement fountain for the front flowerbed because a fountain flows with living water.

Now that it is summer at Maplehurst, I am being confronted by the limits of metaphor. Or perhaps I am confronting my own limits. I plunge my arms into a deep farmhouse sink. I swirl green beans, carrots, a rainbow of Swiss chard, and heads of broccoli so richly green they are nearly purple. In every moment I can spare, I am harvesting, washing, blanching, freezing, eating, feeding. The kitchen garden we rushed to build and plant in spring has itself become a fountain. Between the abundance of rain and the explosion of good things to eat, that word *fountain* is literal, not a metaphor at all.

Metaphor has been more than a pair of eyeglasses to me; it has been my preferred tool for maintaining distance between my own world and the spiritual world. I have used it to say here is my real life and here is the real world, and way over there? Can you see them off in the distance? Those are the promises of God. They speak to us in the language of everyday life, but they do not live in our everyday world.

But they do. The things of God are *here*. The things of God are *now*. And God's fulfilled promises are so real, we can serve them on a platter.

In my Bible, I can point out an inky smear of a date. Also, a little scribble of a star. They remind me that years ago in the wilderness, I heard God say this to me: "they will make gardens and eat their fruit." Those words felt like a promise, and I held on to them through two very unfruitful years. In other words, I believed them. Yet, this summer, I am realizing that I believed them in a hazy, over-spiritualized kind of way. What if God means exactly what he says?

I am elbow-deep in zucchini noodles when I remember God's words in Isaiah: "See, the former things have taken place, and new things I declare; before they spring into being I announce them to you" (Isa. 42:9). God spoke to me of gardens and fruit, long before I saw them with my own eyes. I received his words then in the only way possible. As metaphors and images and dreams. But now time has been fulfilled. We have made a garden, and we are eating its fruit. Just as God said.

He promised, and I eat his words. I sauté them in oil and garlic. I roast them at high heat. I shred them and peel them into ribbons. I toss them in salads and share them with neighbors. They are delicious. Beyond anything I dreamed when I ordered those seeds one dark January night. And far, far beyond anything I saw when I first scribbled that ballpoint star.

The rich abundance of July is sweet, but it isn't only sweet. My children are home from school, and though I love to have them near, our togetherness has left me drowning. Drowning in more than rain or vegetables. I am a highly sensitive and introverted mother of four small but loud children. I have a husband who travels. I am a battery being wound down with every touch and sound and conversation, but it is summer and there is no way for this battery to recharge.

It is a season of too much: too much humidity, too much rain, and too much noise. Yet I recognize that there is another way to tell this same story. Because there is also too much zucchini in the garden, too much basil in the plot near my kitchen door. There is too much time for reading on the porch and too much time for doing absolutely nothing at all.

My children have too many books checked out from the library, the baby is crawling much too fast, and at dusk, when I lock the chickens in their coop, there are too many fireflies to count. I turn in a slow circle, and they are everywhere, a Milky Way of twinkling stars against the dark sky of trees and grass.

In April, I underlined these words in my Bible: "I will make them and the places surrounding my hill a blessing. I will send down showers in season; there will be showers of blessing" (Ezek. 34:26). In May, I bought a rain gauge for the vegetable garden. By the end of June, our little corner of Pennsylvania had broken an all-time record for rainfall.

God means just what he says. How easily I forget that the things of God are not spiritual abstractions. They are the very real things of this world. As real as raindrops.

The kids and I were caught in the rain earlier this week. I wanted to run with Elsa in the shelter of my arms, but three children trailed behind me through the parking lot, and I imagined passing motorists might frown at the mother who leaves her ducklings to their own devices. We walked the slow pace of Beau's four-year-old legs, but the drops turned sharp and cold. Worried, I looked toward my baby girl, but I didn't find a look of discomfort. Instead, she had tilted her face back and up. Her eyes were wide open, and she looked interested. Unafraid.

I followed her lead. I turned my face up to welcome the sharpness and the coldness. "This," I told her, "is a shower of blessing."

This Path Is a Place

Blessed are those . . . whose hearts are set on pilgrimage.

Psalm 84:5

Five acres sounds like a lot. At least, it always has to me. In reality, it is small enough to fit within a glance. If I want, I can take in nearly the whole property from only a few windows. Through the north-facing windows in the two rooms belonging to Elsa and the boys, my eyes can follow the full sweep of the grass from the front porch to the country road. If I move from the southern and western windows in my room to the eastern windows in Lillian's, my eyes can trace the entire curve of the houses that ring us in.

Five acres is large, but it is not endless. Today, standing near the western loop of the fence, I can still hear Beau and Thaddeus all the way on the other side of the house. They are arguing over a stick. Five acres is sometimes not big enough. Yet here we are, Jonathan and I, somehow carving out a sense of the infinite.

It began with a practical, pressing need. My father recently came for a visit. Within five minutes of stepping outside, he was identifying vast hordes of slick, green poison ivy leaves. Once we followed his pointing finger, we could see it here, here, here, everywhere, almost. As if a single vine had for years wandered unchecked in the shadow of the split-rail fence.

Now every time the boys push through the screen door to embark on yet another epic adventure, someone yells after them, "Watch out for poison ivy!" Jonathan and I are both in dread of rash-covered children, which is why, in gloves, cotton pants, and long sleeves, we are filling large kitchen trash bags with malicious vines.

As the vines begin to give way, our work takes on another dimension. Now we are not only eradicating, we are creating. Gradually, we are forging a meandering path between the belt of trees and the fence. Along the way, I find just the spot for a hammock. I imagine it swinging between a dogwood tree and a pine. I also find a few old azaleas and a forgotten rambling rose. And so, our five acres grow.

When we moved a few years ago from a city apartment to a suburban house, our new patch of lawn felt like a vast possession. Jonathan purchased his first push mower with fear and trepidation. We were intimidated by the green perfection of the neighboring yards, but we loved telling the kids to go outside.

In those days, the thought of five acres would have seemed both overwhelming and too good to be true. With five acres, I could grow every single plant I had ever admired. Five acres or one hundred and five. Compared to my little fenced-in postage stamp, they would have seemed to me much the same. Endless.

Yet even with five acres, itself more than I can yet manage, let alone cultivate, I resent the boundaries. My eyes seek out the deficiencies. If five acres can be gathered with a glance, then I focus too often on what that glance does not find. I wish we had a creek, bubbling across some corner. I wish we had a small pond, just big enough for a family of ducks. I wish for a wider hedge of trees between our property and the neighbors'.

Even the chickens appear to want to live beyond their means. Free to roam every one of these acres, they make a mad dash for our next-door neighbor's bird feeder every single time I open the door to their run. We are all such funny birds. We will rush to the far side of a golden meadow just to yearn for the greener grass beyond.

I am a home-loving homebody, but even for me staying put is not easy. I read travel guides and travel memoirs, and I love the travel section of the Sunday paper. We live far from family and still haven't found a babysitter, but that doesn't stop me from dreaming of weekends away. Probably we should at least aim for an occasional date night, but I am bewitched by the dazzling impossibility of a B and B in New England or a slow meander up to Quebec.

But there are the chickens to be fed, the baby to be held, the garden to be weeded, and I must tread carefully lest my daydreams turn these daily gifts into resentments. I imagine some are called across far miles as they follow the way that is Jesus. Their feet will carry good news to place after place after place. But I am called to walk a way that is more like a spiral. My path lies entirely within the long loop of this vine-covered fence. It is a labyrinth rather than a highway.

Christian pilgrims have always emphasized the journey above the destination. This was true for Chaucer's Canterbury pilgrims, and it was true for my friend's mother who recently walked the famous Camino de Santiago in Spain. Yet in our hurried, goal-oriented world, we speak well of pilgrimage but too easily lose sight of its defining quality. It is the *way* of pilgrimage that matters most.

At Maplehurst, that truth is harder to forget. Every day, I wake knowing two things. I know that I have already arrived, and I know there are more miles to travel on this day. I am living an adventure in stability. Mine is a pilgrimage in one place.

The world God has allotted to each of us can never be summed up with a glance. No matter its size. It is God's presence that makes a place endless. This is true whether we are speaking of our souls or of our backyards. God holds the cosmos in his hands, and we hold God within our bodies. There is always more to see.

***

Jonathan and I clear a sheltered spot within a half circle of azaleas. I vaguely remember that spring brought dashes of white and magenta to this shadowy corner, but the blooms must have been half-hidden by vines. While I imagine what this newly cleared spot will look like next spring, Jonathan says he thinks this is just the place for a fire pit. When we slice up some of these fallen logs, we will have ready-made seats. We can ask the boys to attack them with sandpaper.

We each lower ourselves on a log, to rest, to drink from our dripping water bottles, and to appreciate our progress. This northwest corner of the hill is lower than the space where the house sits. Seated here, I look up toward the house, and my eyes blink back the sun that glitters from the second-story windows. This is a view I have never seen before. Everything looks a little bigger, wider, higher. Sitting low to the ground, I appreciate how much sky there is. I can see how near we always are to that endless golden blue.

The universe is vast, but it is filled with paths. Like the deep grooves worn by the sun and moon and stars. Like the currents of the sea. Even this seemingly insignificant trail between the fence and the trees. Some days I feel small. On other days, my world feels small. Neither feeling is true. We are infinite creatures living in an infinite cosmos, and we are seen. We are known. We are never forgotten or so lost that we cannot be found.

Whether we pilgrimage through places or within one five-acre plot, our faith is always the faith of the pilgrim. This faith knows there is a welcome prepared for us. There are arms waiting to receive us. And one day each of us will hear a familiar voice and familiar words. We will hear our Maker say, "Well done."

Singing, Together, over the Sea

In his great mercy he has given us new birth into a
living hope.

1 Peter 1:3

I never intended to plant a flower garden. Vegetables seemed like
more than enough, especially while the raised beds and the picket
fence remained only a sketch on a bit of torn graph paper. But I was
tempted by those antique roses in a catalog. They were separated
from the tomato seeds by only a few pages. I did not seek them
out. You might even say they came to me.

Next to come were a few seed packets of zinnias, cosmos, sunflowers, and marigolds. When I ordered them, I thought of annual
flowers only as an extension of the vegetable garden. They would
attract pollinators. They would deter unwelcome insects. Tucked in
and around the vegetables, they would help me to grow more food.

But then, in late spring, my sister came for a visit. In the evenings, we flipped through my gardening books, and she told me

187

about everything she had grown, or tried to grow, in her North Carolina yard. She told me, especially, about dahlias. "Dahlias!" she swooned. "So easy! So beautiful!"

Apparently, if given all summer to grow, dahlias will start flowering just when the zinnias and marigolds begin to grow tired. If I didn't plant dahlias this spring I would have to wait a whole year to try again. Not exactly now or never, but it felt close enough. I ordered eight dahlia tubers through the mail. I had no idea where I would put them.

This is sometimes how a work of art begins. Through accident and contingency. A whispered encouragement. A spur-of-the-moment decision.

The dahlia tubers arrived toward the end of May. They looked like old, pale sweet potatoes. I laid them out on the grass, and then I began bringing up from the basement all of the flower seedlings I had not managed to squeeze into the vegetable beds, which was, truthfully, most of the flowers I had grown. I am not sure where I thought they would go when I started so many seeds back in March.

I first thought of planting everything in the circular flowerbed. They could fill in the empty space where I still had not replaced the fountain. But I worried that six-foot-tall dahlias, zinnias, and cosmos in that spot where the driveway branches might make it even harder for visitors to find their way to our front door.

As it is, our looping driveway confuses those making their first visit. I try to keep the porch near the front door clear of toys and muddy shoes, but, too often, I hear a knock on the back door, which opens into the rear of the front hall. Most of our first-time guests shuffle their way into the house between a pile of discarded rain boots and an awkwardly placed radiator. Jonathan and I are thinking about planting a little wooden arrow into the ground of the circular flowerbed. It would point toward the right and, we hope, lead visitors to the front door on the western side of the house.

Though it is a looping circle, in my mind the driveway points in only one direction. It points toward home. Always. It will forever be my road back. My way of return. But sometimes I flip through the pages of our guest book and all the names and all the scribbled notes we have gathered in this first year remind me that Maplehurst also sits at a crossroads. For some, this hilltop is a place to pause on their journey. A place to rest along the way. For others, the circular drive is a road for setting forth. It is the point from which to begin again.

But I want Maplehurst to be more than a place for rest and reorientation. And I want it to be more than my home. More than simply a gift given to me. I bear the image of the great Creator, and I want Maplehurst to be my creation. My work of art. My offering.

Where does art come from? Like so many of the very best things in this world, its roots spread through emptiness and brokenness. Art begins when someone recognizes that things are not as they should be. Our art is born in the ache between death and resurrection, and we make art in the empty hours between Friday and Sunday.[1] Whether we speak of poems or paintings or places, all art acknowledges an absence and dreams of something other, something more. Art is the material form of hope.

Art is also an argument. A method of persuasion. I want Maplehurst to embody welcome, but I hope it can also be a challenge. For those grown accustomed to hurry and stress, Maplehurst will shout, *There is another way to live!* For those who have forgotten that the earth is their home, Maplehurst will whisper, *This is where you belong.* For those who feel lost, I hope this house reminds them that all of life is a journey of return.

Jonathan and I cannot force these messages, but we can cultivate them the way I cultivate the garden. And we can let them slip through our fingers like water, pour from our hearts like a fountain, and pray that they echo even in the noisy day-to-day reality of family life.

Ours is a waiting world. But what will we grow in the emptiness? What will we cultivate with the moments and resources given to us? I want to grow a living hope. Something as vivid and as alive as a bed of flowers. I want to create something that shows the way. A signpost of the good things God has planned for us and our world. Like an arrow planted in the very place where we anticipate a fountain.

Yesterday I filled an ironstone pitcher with cosmos, zinnias, and marigolds. The cosmos and marigolds are white. The zinnias are Benary's Giant in salmon rose. Today I can see a fine dusting of pollen on my kitchen counter. There also seems to be pollen in the fruit bowl. But I suppose the art I am most interested in creating has more to do with enchantment than perfection. It is candlelight, rather than clean floors. A table that spills over with good food, rather than just-scrubbed countertops.

Today I am on my knees deadheading marigolds. The cosmos are waving their lacy green fingers over my sunhat and spraying my shoulders with dew. The heavy heads of the zinnias are nodding, nodding, nodding, like buoys lifting and dropping on waves. I know that it is only a flowerbed, but it feels, for a moment, like the sea.

Since the beginning, God's spirit has hovered over the waters. But sometimes, I am there too. Then I hear the hymn of creation and know that the three-fold voice has never stopped singing. And I join in.

Dreams in Black and White

I will see the goodness of the LORD in the land of
the living.

Psalm 27:13

I am always shocked by how real life is. How hot the summer air
feels on my arms. How wet the rain is in my hair. How quickly a
few zucchini vines tumbled on the compost pile can fill my nose
with the smell of rot and decay. Right now, the air in my kitchen
is thick, and I am drowning in the simmering scent of a Crock-Pot
full of garden tomatoes.

I can feel a trickling line of sweat slipping down the side of my
neck, just behind my ear. It tickles the mosquito bites I wear like
a necklace. I study the dirt smudged on the backs of my hands.
There is a black half-moon beneath each fingernail. I do not like
sweat or dirt. Right now, I am not even sure if I like tomatoes.
I sometimes wish I could live in dreams rather than a real world
where dreams come true.

I long for a shower and the cool sheets of my bed, but August
days are long and sunset is still hours away. Maybe that is the

greatest gift of sleep. Seven or eight hours in which to forget that we have bodies. But then I remember that in my most terrifying and frequent nightmare, I have a body that will not move. A body like a lump of Play-Doh. Legs that cannot run. Our bodies can feel like burdens even in sleep.

No wonder we seek escape. We hop in the car, we board a plane, we move, move, move. Maybe we turn on a computer and dive into the internet. There is a reason we call it *cyberspace* and not *cyberplace*. In the no-place that is the online world, we can seek relief from the weight of our bodies. We may try to escape our responsibility to a particular place. And we sometimes find a momentary freedom, floating on a sea of newness and endless choice, untethered by webs of relationship.

Of course, we were never meant to live that way. We are more like trees than birds. The meaning of our lives can only be discovered in our roots. What ties us to the ground and where? How are we bound to other people? Hardly less important is the question weighing heaviest on my mind right now: What should I make for dinner?

How will I feed all the beautiful, hungry mouths about to enter this kitchen? I asked the big kids to take a break from the sunshine and Slip'N Slide with an afternoon viewing of *The Wizard of Oz*, but I am running out of time. I can hear Dorothy's plaintive cry, "There's no place like home."

I can't imagine turning on the oven. I don't want to add a single ambient degree to this south-facing, unair-conditioned kitchen. But we not only live in places, we make them. Even if it is only the place that is our family dinner table.

I may not like dirt, especially when it is stubbornly caked around my fingernails or dragged across my kitchen floor, but there is no escaping it. Trying to escape the dirt makes as much sense as trying to escape our own selves. Our own flesh. But of course we try. We do try.

Without dirt, without fertile soil, our dreams would only tease us with impossibilities. We must plant our dreams in real earth. We must dirty our hands. It's the only way. Whether we dream of planting flower gardens or churches, every dream needs a place in which to take root and grow. Every dream needs a home.

We came home to Maplehurst and brought all our dreams with us. All the dreams already dreamed, and every dream still to come. We will never stop dreaming. There is no living apart from dreaming. I believe this ground is fertile enough for every dream that will be given to us. "Where there is no revelation, people cast off restraint" (Prov. 29:18). Without the dreams of God to keep us rooted, we are lost.

I love my dreams, but I often resent my dreams come true. They are too real, too messy, too complicated. They are four little people asking for food, night after night after night. Four little people who do not like tomatoes. In August, there is little but tomatoes.

So, tomatoes it shall be. I wash my hands three times before I fill a skillet with garlicky stewed tomatoes from the Crock-Pot. I add a can of well-washed white beans. I leave it simmering while I dash back out to the garden for a few long, ruffled leaves of Swiss chard. I tear off the bug-eaten edges before I cut out the stems and ribs.

It seems a shame not to use these rainbow-colored stems, but I am aiming for speed. I set them aside. I guess the chickens will eat rainbows tomorrow. I slice the tender leaves, then stir them in. I crack six eggs into this tomato nest and watch through the glass dome of the lid as they cook, sunny-side-up. The goal, I decide, is to cook them long enough that they won't cause my children to gag but not so long that they won't make a sauce when broken open.

I call everyone to the table as I move the skillet to a trivet. This dish is a mess, but, somehow, it still smells delicious. It looks and smells like Maplehurst in August. It is the knock-you-down smell of simmering tomatoes. It is the shocking orange of our own egg yolks. It is vivid and intense. Dreams realized in a single, Technicolor dish.

One child gags. One child never takes a bite. One child aims to earn the approval her siblings have squandered and says, "It's okay." Elsa eats bowl after bowl, the warm juice running red rivers down her arms. Neither Jonathan nor I can decide exactly what to call this skillet meal, but we call it good. And we eat our fill.

My dream-come-true home has no central air-conditioning. Window units in the bedrooms buzz when we are desperate, but for the most part we rely on portable fans. Occasional breezes. Closed windows and thick brick walls when it is especially hot.

But I have realized something. As much as I would love to flick a switch and fill my house with refrigerated air, I know now what we would lose. We may be the only ones in the neighborhood who notice the precise moment when the evening breeze begins to blow. First, we hear it. The leaves at the tops of the trees announce its coming. The coloring pages my children have left lying on the porch begin to rustle.

These sounds draw us out onto the porch after dinner. Jonathan and I rock side by side in our chairs, lulled by the hum and buzz of a neighborhood of air conditioners. The children turn cartwheels in the grass, and Elsa claps her hands. We talk about chickens and children. Swiss chard rainbows and harvest moons.

I decide that *The Wizard of Oz* gets it exactly backward. It is our dreams that are black and white. Waking life is almost too colorful to bear, but it is our home. This is the land of the living.

Roots to Remember and Branches to Dream

But I am like an olive tree flourishing in the house of God.

Psalm 52:8

I tend to think of seasons as four separate compartments to the year. Like nesting boxes in graduated sizes. But they are more like the LEGO blocks in my son's latest creation. Interlocking and over-lapping. Difficult to pry apart. More than the sum of their parts.

I am standing over the kitchen sink in order to eat a peach from a local orchard. The juice is streaming down my right arm. It is like a sunset, melting. I hold the fading summer sun in my hand and watch gray clouds hauling themselves briskly across a sky that foreshadows autumn. A few yellow cherry leaves somersault across the grass.

I tend to think of prayer the same way. Like the paper trays Jonathan keeps on his desk upstairs. There is the inbox and the outbox. There is a spot marked *urgent* and one for the less pressing

195

overflow. If I think long enough, I can assign each prayer a neat label. *Answered. Unanswered. Ongoing. Expires in five days.* The paper trail of prayer is clearly defined. Requests move in one direction. Responses in the other.

But of course prayer is nothing like a paper tray. Of course, of course, it is so much more like standing beneath an autumn sky while you hold summer in your hand. The truly astonishing thing about prayer is not that our prayers are sometimes answered. The thing that never fails to startle me, to wake me up and scatter the paper piles of my mind, is that *even the prayers themselves are given.*

Here is the prayer like one falling leaf. Here is the answer like the taste of this golden peach.

It is late August and Maplehurst suddenly looks familiar. Month after month of newness and strangeness have brought me back around to something I have seen before. Once again, we are cocooned within a thick, green hedge of maple leaves. Once again, the cherry trees scatter their leaves like overeager flower girls at a wedding. Again, the sticky weight of summer feels immovable before it is suddenly blown aside by a chill murmuring through the screen door. I have listened to these murmurings before.

This August marks an end. Like every true end, it is also a beginning. I seem to be looking back and looking ahead in equal measure. Remembering. Anticipating. Watching as the lines between yesterday, today, and tomorrow begin to blur. It seems that time, on the surface such a rational, logical sequence, cannot be separated into paper trays either.

Lillian and I have been talking about a birthday party. In September she will turn ten. Four days later, Elsa will turn one. When we talk about the party (*Is one party okay? Do you want to share a birthday cake or have your own?*), we also talk about the past, and we talk about prayer.

We remember all those years when she made the same request every night as I tucked her into bed. "Please, Mom, can't I have a sister?" And we remember the night I finally told her, not a little impatiently, that only Jesus gives sisters, so maybe she should talk to him about it. And we remember that she did. We smile and remember even as the answer to that prayer walks our way, scraping a kitchen chair across the tiles for balance.

Why does Scripture echo with the twin commands to *return* and *remember*? It is because God's promises always intersect with places. We relate to God and to one another in some place. To remember is to return. To return is to remember. Rootlessness is a kind of forgetting. And home is the dwelling place of memory.

Today, as we plan a birthday party, I remember how God gave my daughter a prayer, and that he did it through my own hasty, impatient mouth. And I remember that when God answered my daughter's prayer, he also gave me the unacknowledged desire of my heart.

When we remember and return, we live as we were meant to live. We live like trees, nourished by streams of water. Unfortunately, our common idea of a tree is incomplete. We think tree, and we imagine a trunk with branches when really we should see a trunk with great branching structures at both ends. Any gardener who has ever given thought to a tree's drip line knows that its branches are mirrored underground by its roots. If we are trees, then memories are our roots. Our limbs are our dreams, reaching for their source in heaven.

Trees seem to hold all four seasons within themselves, revealing in turn bud, leaf, color, bare branch. Perhaps it is the same with us. We, too, are made up of so many hidden things. Seasons, stories, places, and people. We, too, depend absolutely on the sky, the earth, and all that is alive around us.

197

Our identities are always relational, just as God's identity is relational. Who is God? He is the three-in-one. He is love. And who I am can never be untangled from the children born to me. Who I am can never be separated from this home. As for my daughters, some part of their identities will always remain rooted in their relationship to one another. They will always be older sister and younger sister. The one who asked and the one who was given.

———

Lillian decides on two cakes. I should have seen that coming. No child of mine would choose one cake if two were being offered. First, we will have a vanilla cake with whipped cream and blackberries. Four days later, in honor of Elsa and the new season knocking on our door, we will have a cream-cheese apple cake with a crumbly cinnamon-sugar top. Thaddeus, bless his heart, will have his own chocolate cupcakes from the gluten-free bakery.

The apple cake is from a recipe I started using when I was a newlywed, years before I became a mother. I've tasted it dozens of times. But I imagine it will be different this year. This time it will carry the scent of the spring blossoms on our own small apple trees. It will taste of apples from the orchard on the other side of town. And it will also taste of the apples we will harvest from our trees in all the years to come. It will taste like memory. It will taste like a dream.

All the Loose Ends
in the Sky

Holy, holy, holy is the LORD Almighty; the whole earth
is full of his glory.

Isaiah 6:3

A sudden gust of real wind blows through the oscillating fan I
keep wedged on the windowsill in the kitchen. The blades of the
fan buzz. Elsa's sweaty curls lift and dance. All the papers I have
organized with magnets on the refrigerator door fly toward the
ceiling before drifting slowly into the corners of the room.

I scramble to collect the chore charts I printed with such enthusiasm in June, but my elbow knocks the jam jar filled with gold star
stickers. Ignoring the stars, I gather up the summer reading lists
from the library. I return the crayon masterpieces to their front-of-
fridge place of honor. We are still reading, but we stopped filling
out the lists sometime around the fourth of July.

The calendar says summer will reign for a few more weeks yet,
but I wonder how much more I can take. End-of-summer life is so

messy. So sweaty. So full. It defies all my instincts for neatness and order, for control, and for the checking off of lists.

Late-August days are like these star stickers. I intended them to march in rows across our charts, but now they sparkle among the dust bunnies. When Beau suddenly runs through the screen door, gold stars shine from the bottoms of his dirty feet.

I never have outgrown my kindergarten love for shiny gold stars in neat rows. But it is harder to find them now. I used to earn stars for making my bed or putting the crayons back where they belong. And I still love order and efficiency. I have always excelled at following directions. Coloring in the lines. In me is still the firstborn daughter ambitious for approval and admiration. I work all day trying to gather up the loose ends of our summer lives, but no one is handing out stars.

I lean over the heat of my sauté pan, push a wooden spoon through bright yellow squash, gold oil, and browned bits of garlic. There is no gold star when I entice my children to eat their vegetables. No gold star when I remember to sweep the kitchen floor. Yet Paul told Jesus's first followers that humble lives, emptied of selfish ambition, would shine "like stars in the sky" (Phil. 2:15). And he gave them this surprising charge: "Make it your ambition to lead a quiet life" (1 Thess. 4:11).

I no longer remember what I thought of Paul's strange words before I came to Maplehurst. But for twelve months I have witnessed the glory of a quiet life. I am beginning to understand what it might mean to be ambitious for quietness rather than accomplishment. I still do not live this quietness every day, perhaps not even on most days, but I am sure it is the thing most worthy of all my ambition. The quiet life shares the good news loudest, perhaps because only the quiet life is first able to hear the good news.

And I have seen, too, that a quiet life is not inevitable. It is not the default in this world. We may sometimes find ourselves in a very quiet place. Often, the road of suffering will carry us there despite our unwillingness to go. But nearly all of us must work to stay there. All the energies of the flesh, all the vanity of a world that has rejected heaven, seem bent on making noise. Bent on leading us away from the quiet life that sings so beautifully of the world that is to come.

Stars belong in the sky, and dirt belongs underfoot. But the wonderful, maddening truth is that creation's order is like the order of an overfull cup. Contained yet spilling out. Stars live in the sky, but they also shoot, explode, fall. Why should I be surprised to find them in the dirty corners of my kitchen floor?

I would have limited God's glory to sunsets and rainbows. To the color of dahlias and the taste of peaches. But in August I understand that the earth is full of his glory. It soaks everything, seeps from every seam. It spills out in a sudden wind. It burns our skin like sunshine. We droop beneath the heavy weight of glory in the humid air and spy its mystery in the spider that scuttles away before we quite know what it is we've seen.

According to Isaiah, the angels don't sing about heaven. They sing about earth: "Holy, holy, holy is the LORD Almighty; the whole earth is full of his glory" (Isa. 6:3). This is glory that can't be gathered up, like all the loose ends of our daily lives. Perhaps there is glory in those piles of LEGOs we left to lie in the middle of the floor when we went to bed yesterday. Perhaps glory even in the popcorn we ate for dinner last night because it was too hot to cook.

In summer, loose ends don't only scatter like papers in the wind. They also twist and curl and dance. Like pea vines on a lattice. Or morning glories on the porch. They call us out, far beyond the known boundaries of the world that is. They tempt us to stay up past our bedtimes. They beckon us to look deeply at spiderwebs and the freckles on our little boy's nose. They gleam and hover like fireflies. We try to catch them but do not really mind when we fail and our fists close over emptiness.

Quietness is a receptive emptiness. Only the meek will inherit the earth because only the meek have room within themselves to receive such a wide and wild inheritance. At Maplehurst I have seen where the gold stars shine. They are not found in finishing chores or checking off lists. Not in hustle or efficiency. They glow in unexpected places, like the ends of every loose, twisting strand of a baby girl's hair.

But gold stars can also be found just where they are meant to be. The true tragedy of an unquiet life is not that we are unable to find the stars that fall to unexpected corners. The greatest tragedy is that we do not even slow down long enough to find the stars where we know they can be found.

I want nothing less than the stars. And so I risk handing my stack of fragile dinner plates to a small boy. I pile golden squash and sliced tomatoes on platters. I stop worrying whether or not my children will turn tonight's BLT sandwiches into a dinner of bacon only. And together we pour out of the steamy kitchen and on toward the cool of the porch. Lillian drags the heavy highchair along like an anchor.

We eat every last crumbled bit of bacon. When Jonathan slides warm peach halves from the grill, we spoon vanilla ice cream into the hollow left by the pit. Beau leaves the skin of his peach in a little puddle on the table, but he lowers his face and licks every drop of ice cream from his plate.

Elsa falls asleep on Jonathan's shoulder, but I am in no rush to carry her upstairs. Instead, I watch the kids lean over the porch rails, blowing bubbles through plastic wands. Each one is like a day in summer. They grow and swell until their rainbow skin shimmers. The evening breeze carries them up and away and on toward a sky just beginning to spill gold stars. Beneath the sky is an earth so richly quiet, I can hear the trees sing.

Notes

This Place Marked by a Star

1. Find more on Epiphany and house blessings in Kimberlee Conway Ireton's book *The Circle of Seasons* (Downers Grove, IL: InterVarsity, 2008). Ireton has adapted this prayer from Gertrud Mueller Nelson's *To Dance with God: Family Ritual and Community Celebration* (Mahwah, NJ: Paulist Press, 1986).

A House of Brick and Symbol

1. Craig G. Bartholomew, *Where Mortals Dwell* (Grand Rapids: Baker Academic, 2011), 99.

An Ancient Song, Always New

1. Alexander Schmemann, *For the Life of the World* (Yonkers, NY: St. Vladimir's Seminary Press, 1973), 16.

Singing, Together, over the Sea

1. George Steiner, *Real Presences* (Chicago: University of Chicago Press, 1991), 231–32.

Christie Purifoy has been a regular contributor for a variety of on-line sites, including *Grace Table*, *Pick Your Portion*, and *A Deeper Story* and has contributed essays to numerous other websites, including *Art House America* and well-known blogs by Lisa-Jo Baker, Jennifer Dukes Lee, and Ann Voskamp. Christie has a PhD in English Literature from the University of Chicago and has taught literature and composition to undergraduates at the University of Chicago, the School of the Art Institute of Chicago, and the University of North Florida.

In 2012, Christie traded the university classroom for a large vegetable garden and a henhouse in southeastern Pennsylvania. When the noise of her four young children makes writing impossible, she tends zucchini and tomatoes her children will later refuse to eat. The zucchini-loving chickens are perfectly happy with this arrangement. The chickens move fast and the children even faster, but Christie is always watching for the beauty, mystery, and wonder that lie beneath it all. When she finds it, she writes about it at her blog, *There Is a River* (www.christiepurifoy.com).

VISIT CHRISTIEPURIFOY.COM

Made in the USA
Las Vegas, NV
02 August 2022

52584873R10115